OKRs
FOR
ALL

OKRs FOR ALL

Making Objectives and Key Results work for your Entire Organization

Vetri Vellore

WILEY

Library of Congress Cataloging-in-Publication Data:

Names: Vellore, Vetri, author.
Title: OKRs for all : making objectives and key results work for your entire organization / Vetri Vellore.
Description: Hoboken, New Jersey : Wiley, [2023] | Includes index.
Identifiers: LCCN 2022012508 (print) | LCCN 2022012509 (ebook) | ISBN 9781119811596 (cloth) | ISBN 9781119811626 (adobe pdf) | ISBN 9781119811602 (epub)
Subjects: LCSH: Management by objectives. | Strategic planning. | Goal setting in personnel management.
Classification: LCC HD30.65 .V45 2022 (print) | LCC HD30.65 (ebook) | DDC 658.4/012—dc23/eng/20220511
LC record available at https://lccn.loc.gov/2022012508
LC ebook record available at https://lccn.loc.gov/2022012509

Cover Design: Wiley

SKY10035998_091322

Contents

Introduction

There's a parable about three bricklayers that has always captured the importance of purpose-driven work for me.

A man walking down the street sees three bricklayers. Each of them is diligently placing bricks along a wall, and each of them is working very hard.

To the first bricklayer, the man asks the question, "What are you doing?" The bricklayer replies, "I am laying bricks. I am working hard to feed my family."

The man moves to the second bricklayer and asks the same question, "What are you doing?" to which the second bricklayer replies, "I'm building this nice, big wall."

Finally, the man comes to the third bricklayer, who is the most focused, and asks again, "What are you doing?" The third one has a gleam in his eye and says, "I'm building a great cathedral."

The fact is, most employees don't know why they're doing the work they do; they just work on what their manager tells them to or what some project management tool lists as the next task for them.

When every team and person in your organization is aligned to the strategic priorities of the business and understands the purpose behind their work, they are highly engaged, productive, and happy. It's true when building cathedrals, and it's true in business.

Businesses today face constant disruption and uncertainty—whether due to technical disruptions, market changes, financial conditions, war, or pandemics upending whole industries. These businesses need a new framework to move the business forward, pivot when necessary, and empower their teams.

When teams understand the "why" of a company's objectives, they intuitively recognize concepts and plans more concretely, and will be able to flag risks, changes needed, and opportunities that may have been missed otherwise.

By focusing on what matters in the midst of the daily whirlwind of activity, your teams stay in the "flow" and are highly productive. Purpose and alignment bring your teams together and foster collaboration.

The leadership challenge is how to bring purpose to the work everyone is doing, so everyone in the organization understands that they are building a cathedral and not just coming to work every day to lay bricks one at a time.

I've seen thousands of businesses drive alignment, purpose, and focus and increase business resilience and growth by leveraging the goal methodology of objectives and key results (OKRs). In the following pages, you'll learn how this can be accomplished for you and your business as well.

Why Now?

In March of 2020, COVID-19 tore across the globe and upended life as we knew it. Like most business leaders, I closed my company's office and sent the team to work from home, unsure of when we'd come back or what the pandemic meant for our business's future (at least those of us fortunate enough to work in industries where we could do so). At the time, we hoped it would be only a few weeks. Then, a few weeks turned into our new normal. Our entire way of working changed.

While the shift to hybrid and remote work appears to have happened in blink of an eye, the shift has been underway for years. Over the past decade, more and more employees have opted for flexible work arrangements and work hours, and more and more employers have started to embrace this change. Business leaders have been under steadily growing pressure to show success faster and, as our teams move to distributed models, the old systems that worked in-office are creating bottlenecks and leading to a lack of alignment. Talent has become harder to attract and retain than ever. COVID-19 exacerbated these changes, but it did so more quickly than any of us could have imagined.

Businesses are under ever-increasing pressure to quickly adapt to these shifts, while continuing to keep every employee focused, motivated, and driving business outcomes.

I'm excited to share how OKRs can add value to every single employee in your organization and accelerate the business.

My company, Ally.io, which has since been acquired by Microsoft, builds OKR software. This framework has been central to how we operate our business, providing the foundation for every discussion and initiative. In March of 2020, as we all scrambled to make sense of the external factors changing our lives, OKRs helped ground the entire team to our most important work and, more importantly, to the outcomes we needed to drive.

More important than my own experience in using OKRs to grow multiple businesses, my team and I have helped thousands of teams do the same, using OKRs and our software. From large enterprises to startups, technology to manufacturing, media to healthcare, and operations and HR to engineering and sales, I have seen OKRs make an impact in every type of business and function.

Throughout this most recent period of change, and others before it, the OKR framework has been the key to resilience for so many businesses, mine included. It has given us the ability to continue to scale as we moved out of the initial system shock and into the new normal.

Most industries have moved to a global, distributed, and sometimes asynchronous workforce. This phenomenon, coupled with a growing tech stack to accommodate it and increased urgency around the pace of innovation and growth, has led to the need for visibility, alignment, and employee engagement across businesses that are becoming more and more complex.

Our businesses are dealing with an urgent need for speed and agility at scale. All while the increase in remote and distributed work has brought new challenges including the impact this hybrid environment has had on our personal lives. Four key themes have emerged more prominently in this hybrid world:

1. **A lack of alignment is creating bottlenecks:** In many cases, managers and teams aren't aware of what other departments are working on, whether they're focused on the same initiatives, or whether their own group is working on the right initiatives or driving toward the right outcomes. This lack of structure is exacerbated by processes that often rely on a single person or single point of failure. Without the alignment needed to move quickly and in synch, the business can slow to a crawl, create customer-facing problems, or have teams doing duplicate work.

2. **The need for growth and resilience are more daunting than ever:** Almost half (48%) of executives say that the biggest risk to their business achieving its growth targets.[1] The expectations investors and shareholders have for exponential growth are higher than ever, and the competitive landscape

---

[1]PWC Pulse Survey, 2022 https://www.pwc.com/us/en/library/pulse-survey/executive-views-2022.html.

is exploding, regardless of industry or vertical. In fact, 2021 ended with over 832 "unicorn" companies (privately held businesses valued at over $1 billion).[2] In 2015, unicorns numbered fewer than 80. This pressure falls squarely on the shoulders of the leadership team. In 2021, we saw record CEO turnover, nearly double that of 2018.[3]

3. **The Great Resignation:** Employees are leaving their jobs en masse because they are not connected to the company's purpose. In short, they do not feel like their work matters, and role switching takes less of an emotional toll when they don't find that connection around a proverbial water cooler. According to a 2022 Microsoft Worklab report,[4] 43% of the global workforce is considering a job change. Employees aren't connecting face-to-face like they used to. There's no break room, no ping-pong table, no coffeepot to stand around and gossip. Company culture in 2022 comes from a sense of purpose. Employees want to feel connected to the company's mission and vision, they want to know that they're doing work that contributes to that mission, and they want to trust that the work they're doing is the *right* work.

4. **Visibility is more difficult, and silos have emerged:** As a business leader, you need line-of-sight into the focus areas and work being done across the company and the ability to click deeper to understand a trend, growth opportunity, or risk to the business. On the other side of that coin, your employees need

[2] Nicholas Rapp and Jessica Mathews, "Is the 'Unicorn' Boom Turning into a Bubble?" *Fortune*, October 10, 2021, https://fortune.com/longform/unicorn-boom-bubble-pre-ipo-startups-data-map/.

[3] PwC, "CEO Turnover at Record High; Successors Following Long Serving CEOs Struggling According to PwC's Strategy& Global Study," PwC press release, 2019, https://www.pwc.com/gx/en/news-room/press-releases/2019/ceo-turnover-record-high.html.

[4] "Great Expectations: Making Hybrid Work *Work*," Microsoft Annual Work Trend Index Report, 2022, https://www.microsoft.com/en-us/worklab/work-trend-index.

to experience transparency from you that is not as natural as it may have been in-office. Future Forum finds that employees who feel like their leadership team is transparent are twice as likely to feel confident about their company's future.[5]

In the end, it all comes down to a relentless focus on that purpose and making it central to every part of the business.

Creating Purpose-Driven Work for Every Employee

Perhaps my favorite part of the bricklayer parable is that it's rooted in the true story of the famous architect Christopher Wren, who was commissioned to rebuild St. Paul's Cathedral after the great London fire of 1666. Wren understood that truly executing on something amazing takes everyone working toward the same vision and took it upon himself to ensure that the people working on St. Paul's understood that vision.

This is where two critical challenges come into play when thinking about business execution and translating strategy into actual productivity:

1. Many leaders assume their team automatically has the context of what they're building, and automatically sees why their work matters or fits into the overall mission. That context is actually lost quickly when you traverse different levels of the organization. In fact, the consulting firm McKinsey recently asked this question, and found that while 85% of

---

[5] "The Great Executive–Employee Disconnect," Future Forum by Slack, October 2021, https://futureforum.com/wp-content/uploads/2021/10/Future-Forum-Pulse-Report-October-2021.pdf.

executives and upper management said that they feel connected to purpose at work, only 15% of frontline managers and frontline employees agreed. Worse, nearly half of these employees disagreed, compared with fewer executives and upper management.[6]

2. Too often, organizations and leadership have convinced employees that they are the bricklayers. Employees don't feel empowered to engage in conversations about the broader purpose and believe that they aren't entitled to that context. This has a detrimental effect on productivity. That same McKinsey study found that managers and employees who didn't feel that connection to purpose saw significantly lower outcomes (both at work and in their personal lives) than those who did.

Building Cathedrals with OKRs

OKRs help every employee see the cathedrals they are building with each brick they lay. And, just as importantly, they help leaders determine where more focus is needed, which resources are best suited for which job, and how to move quickly without sacrificing quality.

My team and I have worked with thousands of business leaders from Fortune 500 companies to startups, and every department from engineering and product development to sales,

[6]Naina Dhingra, Andrew Samo, Bill Schaninger, and Matt Schrimper, "Help Your Employees Find Purpose—Or Watch Them Leave," McKinsey & Company, April 5, 2021, https://www.mckinsey.com/business-functions/people-and-organizational-performance/our-insights/help-your-employees-find-purpose-or-watch-them-leave#:~:text=Whereas%2085%20percent%20of%20execs,upper%20management%20(Exhibit%202).

marketing, operations, and HR, to implement and operationalize successful OKR programs. This is not an easy thing to do. The OKR framework is simple to conceptualize, and the results can be incredible, but, like any organizational transformation, is not easy and it takes work to make it stick.

Throughout this book, I'll share anecdotes from a variety of these OKR-driven companies across different industries, highlighting the success they've found, obstacles they've overcome, and tips for the next generation of OKR practitioners.

After thousands of interactions, the one thing that has been proven true time and time again is that a business's biggest and most ambitious goals are more achievable when every employee understands them, understands their influence on them, and their ability to make an impact. OKRs create alignment and shared purpose throughout the entire organization. The VP of operations for a fast-growing and well-known software company recently told me, "The more employees we have using OKRs, the better we've become as a business."

Once an organization masters using OKRs correctly, this framework can increase executional velocity and resilience, and drive productivity and engagement across the organization. It will create a cultural shift in the way work is done and make OKRs the steel thread that runs between that work and the company's biggest objectives.

The OKR methodology is a monumentally powerful tool for aligning an organization, but for decades, it's often been misunderstood, and not applied in a way that productively serves the organization, leaving many employees out of the mix. This diminishes the benefit OKRs bring to their organization, thwarting progress and agility.

OKRs have helped thousands of the most successful companies in the world execute and stay ahead of the game for over

50 years. The goal methodology provides focus, accountability, clarity, and purpose, and leaders have embraced their simplicity and structure like no other framework. They can do the same for you and your team, driving growth, alignment, and flexibility at a time you can't afford to live without it.

Who Is This Book For?

If you're a business leader focused on business growth and resilience, and developing a mission-driven, highly engaged workforce, this book is for you. You will learn the key OKR concepts, how to use them effectively in shaping the culture of your organization and driving business outcomes, and practical guidance on how to get the most out of using OKRs.

For department and team leaders focused on ensuring that your team is aligned to the strategic priorities of the company and is engaged and productive, this book will help you learn OKR concepts and provide practical tips on how to use OKRs to drive team engagement and productivity.

For those in human resources/people operations, you will learn how OKRs relate to your HR processes and provide guidance on how to use OKRs help every employee in your organization to know that their work matters and be highly engaged.

For those enthusiastic or merely curious about OKRs, my hope is that you learn the concepts and enable you to drive OKR initiatives for your team or organization to have an outsized impact.

OKRs are about aligning the entire company to a common purpose, and that takes each person understanding what that purpose is and how to bring it to life.

How This Book Is Organized

In the following pages, I'll show you how to make OKRs work for *everyone* in your organization. Throughout this book, I'll address not only how to leverage OKRs for success, but how to avoid the pitfalls so many have run into.

In this four-part book, you'll find guidance, anecdotes, examples, and frameworks that address the common themes, questions, challenges, and successes we've seen from working with thousands of businesses:

Part I: In OKR Foundations, I'll share the basic fundamentals of what OKRs are and how they're structured, and we'll discuss why they've worked, and in some cases, why they haven't.

Part II: In Applying OKR Principles, you'll learn the tactical application of OKRs, starting with defining meaningful objectives, capturing the relevant key results and key initiatives, and then how to align and cascade OKRs throughout your organization.

Part III: In Running the Business with OKRs, we'll define the core business rhythms that need to be updated to ensure OKR success.

Part IV: In Getting Started with OKRs, armed with the framework and the knowledge of the cadence you'll need to operationalize, I'll share how to build your plan and various mechanisms, and how to ensure that the program doesn't fall flat after the first cycle or two.

Throughout, I'll share both data and stories of how successful companies around the world have used OKRs to transform the way they run their business.

This book will be your practical guide to OKRs, creating a culture that is purpose-driven, providing tools for your managers and teams, and giving you the framework to drive not only a successful OKR program but a successful, thriving, and resilient business.

OKR Foundations

In this first part of the book, I will cover the basics of OKRs, including core concepts and structure so that you have a good understanding of the OKR framework.

My personal OKR for this book is:

Objective (Goal): Provide the best practical guide to OKRs relevant to every person in an organization.

I will measure the success of this objective using the following key results.

1: Enable OKR adoption for 1M teams.

2: Earn 4.9 rating for "usefulness" on Amazon.

3: Make 100% of OKR rollouts successful.

I will reach the above outcomes by doing the following key initiatives:

1: Sign with a reputable publisher.

2: Write a practical manuscript.

3: Earn endorsements from other OKR experts.

This framework may seem unfamiliar to you now, but it won't by the end of the next chapter on "Core Concepts," where I will walk you through the OKR fundamentals in detail. Let's dive in.

1

Core Concepts:
What Are OKRs?

In this chapter, I will provide a breakdown of what OKRs are, and how successful businesses use them to address the challenges of visibility and alignment, the need to drive results faster, and improve employee engagement.

What Do OKRs Do?

OKR is a proven goal-setting framework for creating alignment and focus and building a highly productive and engaged work culture to drive your business outcomes.

OKRs align your entire organization to strategy, shifting focus from output—the everyday work of your team—to outcomes, which are the impact of that work. This mindset shift keeps your team highly engaged with a clear sense of purpose and under-standing of how everyone is contributing to forward momentum.

OKRs sit at the intersection between *purpose* and *strategy* and *execution*.

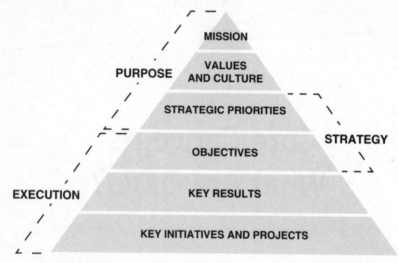

Your mission is the light at the top of your lighthouse, guiding everything you do, closely tied to your values and culture. These make up your organization's purpose.

For instance, if you are a gaming company, your mission (why your business exists) might be "To educate every child using games." Your vision (picture of the future) might be "To make every game an educational game." Your values and culture would reflect this by favoring values like "Educate at every touchpoint" and "Learn every day."

Your strategic priorities, objectives, and key results make up the strategic direction for your organization—they are the outcomes that your organization is hoping to achieve. Your strategic priorities are your go-forward strategy, and your objectives and key results are the connective tissue how you drive the organization to realize your strategic priorities.

Let's go back to our gaming company example, and let's say you are working on a new game. At the company level, your objective isn't to release a new game—it might be to make money for your shareholders. As a business, you may also (and should) have objectives around social impact and doing good in the world, but for the sake of simplicity, let's stick to the revenue objective for now. The projects and key initiatives your engineering team are working on to complete the new game are your output.

Your organization's output is obviously necessary and usually visible, because most employees spend their time in this execution-level work. But the projects and key initiatives itself isn't the desired outcome. It's what you're doing to get to your revenue outcome. This seemingly simple shift in thinking from outputs to outcomes unlocks huge value for an organization.

By pointing your entire team toward outcomes, you enable everyone in the organization to focus on business outcomes instead of projects and activity, empower them to prioritize, and figure out the best ways to get those outcomes. This book gives you an operating manual for getting started with OKRs, the connective tissue between the strategic priorities and everyday work of your team.

OKR Basics: Objectives, Key Results, and Key Initiatives

You can think about objectives, key results, and key initiatives in the following way:

OBJECTIVES: what you want to accomplish
Objectives are clear, inspiring goals. To sharpen focus, limit yourself to five objectives.

KEY RESULTS: how you will measure success
Key results are your measurable outcomes. They should be ambitious but achievable, and quantifiable enough to lead to objective grading. You should have three to five key results.

KEY INITIATIVES: projects and activities which will help achieve outcomes
Key initiatives are the core activities that will drive success of the outcomes defined in your key results.

The formula for writing an OKR is:

OKR FORMULA

I will   OBJECTIVE   as measured by   KEY RESULTS   by doing   KEY INITIATIVES

An objective is directional. Whether at the company, department, or team level, an objective is where you are headed—your target.

Key results are measurable outcomes that signal that you are moving in the right direction toward your objectives.

Key initiatives are the actions your team takes to move key results in the right direction.

Objective: Goals You Want to Accomplish in a Set Period of Time

- **Choose three to five objectives at the most.** This helps you bring focus to your team at every level, from the company-wide OKRs that your leadership puts together to the individual OKRs that your team members put together. Having to pare down all the things you want to accomplish to a list of three to five objectives helps avoid goals from turning into task lists. If you prioritize everything, you prioritize nothing.

  Keep in mind here that you want a mix of objectives that you know you can achieve and ones that you know will be a stretch for you and your organization. This helps create the environment of innovation and creative thinking that OKRs are known for facilitating.

- **Seek simplicity.** Each objective should be clear and concise. This ensures that, as OKRs are made visible throughout your organization, everyone—not just leadership—is able to understand what you are trying to achieve.

- **Ask yourself:** What do you want your organization to accomplish?

Key Results: Expected Outcomes of the Objective

- **Be specific.** Results should be clear, measurable, and not open to subjective interpretation. Use specific numbers and metrics. Binary outcomes, like something got done or not, are not the best—but can be used.
- **Choose three to five key results for each objective.** Too many key results can lead to a lack of focus. OKRs are about providing a spotlight on the most important outcomes, not a floodlight on every outcome. To focus your key results, ask yourself, "Which metrics will *really* show me that I have achieved what I set out to achieve?"
- **Ask yourself:** Does each key result have a clear owner who is accountable for its success? Who do other stakeholders go to when this key result is behind?

Key Initiatives and Projects: These are activities that will be done to achieve the key results.

- **Stay *realistically* optimistic.** Make sure you have the ability (the resources and timeline) to execute the projects and key initiatives under your OKRs. That's what makes an objective realistically optimistic, and not a pipe dream.
- **Ask yourself:** What could get in the way of our projects and key initiatives?

• **Key initiatives are often delegated, and when they are delegated, they can become the objectives or projects of someone else.** This ensures alignment between company-wide OKRs and the work prioritized by every department in your organization. More on this in Part II.

How Objectives, Key Results, and Key Initiatives Fit Together

To explain how objectives, key results, and key initiatives interact with one another, I'm going to use an example.

Let's return to our video game company, and let's say your aspirations are to take over the North American video gaming market. Your objective look like this:

Objective: Become the best gaming platform in North America.

But what does "best" mean? It is first important to clarify what it means to become the best gaming platform in North America, as that could mean different things for different people in the organization. Is becoming the best gaming platform in North America defined by revenue, popularity, users, or something entirely different? You need to be able to objectively measure your outcomes so there is a common, clear understanding across the organization of what you are aiming for, not just what you are doing to get there.

So we add in key results, which explain what "best" actually looks like in terms of results.

Objective: Become the best gaming platform in North America.

- **Key Result:** Achieve 150 million monthly active users.
- **Key Result:** Exceed 90% user retention.

But how will this gaming platform get to the key results that represent success?

This is where we layer in key initiatives, which are the "how" we get to our key results.

Here is the same OKR written with key initiatives in the picture:

Objective: Become the best gaming platform in North America.

- **Key Result:** Achieve 150 million monthly active users.
- **Key Result:** Exceed 90% user retention.
- **Key Initiative:** Ship new version of gaming platform by 6/1 to improve engagement.
- **Key Initiative:** Increase reach of our gaming platform by 10 million new users.

These key initiatives are the work the company needs to do in order to maximize the chance of achieving these key results, and, ultimately, objective. In many cases, these key initiatives need to be tracked and monitored just as closely as the key results.

Your key initiatives and projects are the executional outputs delivered by your team to reach an objective, whereas key results are outcomes that help you measure your progress toward that objective.

Key initiatives and projects are "how you get there," but in differentiated ways.

Key initiatives begin at the company level, beneath objectives and key results. Key initiatives can become objectives for the next level down, the department level. Then the department level's key initiatives become the objectives at the team level. More on this structure, including a visualization, in the next section.

Projects operate at the team and individual level. They are the execution-level, tactical work that needs to get done to achieve all the objectives that come before them.

By bringing key results, key initiatives, and projects together with objectives at the company, department, and team levels, everyone in your organization should have clarity on where they are headed and how they are going to get there.

How OKRs Flow Through an Organization

The ideal state is to have OKRs flow from the business level to departments, teams, and all the way to individuals to enable and align each level to the business priorities.

This might not happen right away—I'll walk you through my phased approach later—but it's where you're headed.

Let's return to the example of our video game company.

Our executive team has come up with a company-wide objective, to become the best gaming platform in North America, which they accomplish via two key results: achieving 150 million monthly active users and exceeding 90% user retention.

They also included two key initiatives, which are how they intend to get to their key results and, ultimately, objective.

Objective: Become the best gaming platform in North America.

- **Key Result:** Achieve 150 million monthly active users.
  - **Key Initiative:** Increase reach of our gaming platform by 10 million new users.
- **Key Result:** Exceed 90% user retention.
  - **Key Initiative:** Ship next version of gaming platform to improve engagement.

But the executive team isn't performing key initiatives on their own. These get delegated out to departments so that the company-wide key initiative of *Ship next version of gaming platform to improve engagement* becomes the product department's objective, with the company-wide key result of exceeding 90% user retention attached to it, and the company-wide key initiative of increasing reach of our gaming platform becoming the marketing department's objective, with the company-wide key result of achieving 150 million monthly active users attached to it.

Each of these departments builds their own key results and new key initiatives to get them to their department-level objective.

I don't want there to be a misunderstanding about the term "delegating" here: OKR creation is a collaborative process in which neither company-wide nor department-wide nor team-level nor individual-level OKRs should be written in isolation or without a dialogue that goes both ways.

From the moment that company-wide OKRs are drafted by your company's top leader, OKRs should facilitate a two-way conversation between leaders and those who report to them about what their objectives and key results should be. This should be a process that exists at every level of your organization. And each department and team should have leeway to choose the "how" they get to where they're headed—their key initiatives. This collaborative approach is the key to OKRs for all.

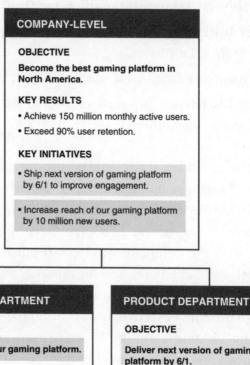

COMPANY-LEVEL

OBJECTIVE
Become the best gaming platform in North America.

KEY RESULTS
• Achieve 150 million monthly active users.
• Exceed 90% user retention.

KEY INITIATIVES
• Ship next version of gaming platform by 6/1 to improve engagement.
• Increase reach of our gaming platform by 10 million new users.

MARKETING DEPARTMENT

OBJECTIVE
Increase reach of our gaming platform.

KEY RESULTS
• Achieve 150 million monthly active users.
• Cost of acquiring new users is less than $100/user.

KEY INITIATIVES
• Release Super Bowl commercial.
• Invest in expansion in three major markets.

PRODUCT DEPARTMENT

OBJECTIVE
Deliver next version of gaming platform by 6/1.

KEY RESULTS
• Exceed 90% user retention.
• Reduce latency by 10%.

KEY INITIATIVES
• Enable group play.
• Deliver high-speed gaming backbone network.

Company Objective:

Become the best gaming platform in North America.

Key Results:

Achieve 150 million monthly active users.

Exceed 90% user retention.

Key Initiatives:

Ship next version of gaming platform to improve engagement [delegated to Product].

Increase reach of our gaming platform [delegated to Marketing].

Marketing Objective:

Increase reach of our gaming platform.

Key Results:

Achieve 150 million monthly active users.

Cost of acquiring new users is less than $100/user.

Key Initiatives:

Release Super Bowl commercial.

Invest in expansion in three major markets.

Product Objective:

Deliver next version of gaming platform by 6/1.

Key Results:

Exceed 90% user retention.

Reduce latency by 10%.

Key Initiatives:

Enable group play.

Deliver high-speed gaming backbone network.

Now let's go to the next level down; the team level. Let's use the product department as an example.

Within the product department, we have the platform team and the infrastructure team. The key initiatives at the product department level are delegated as objectives to the platform and infrastructure teams.

Instead of key initiatives, the platform and infrastructure teams have projects, since they are doing the fundamental, project-level work here and there is no team below them to delegate work to.

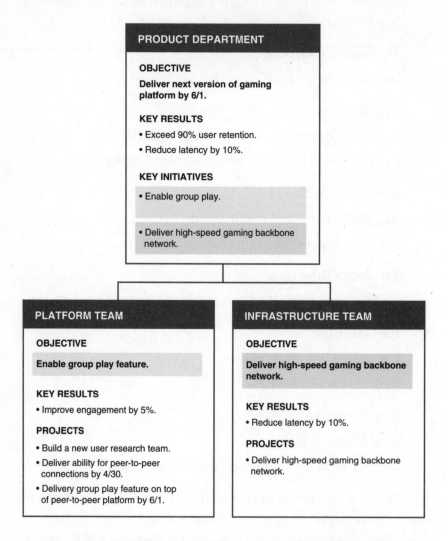

If you are the infrastructure team, you are no longer wondering why you are working on delivering the high-speed gaming network.

You have a clear objective to rally around, understand why it is important (to deliver the next version of gaming platform → increase retention rate of users), and have clarity on what it means to achieve the objective (reducing latency by 10%). Now it's up to your team to put together the project plan for how to achieve your objective.

I have seen companies be most successful when objectives, key results, and key initiatives are first set at the company level. This helps give all departments and teams the directional clarity that makes OKRs so valuable.

That said, this process should not operate like a dictatorship, where OKRs are simply handed down from the top without vetting, questioning, and collaborative input from departments and teams. Why? Because the other piece of what makes OKRs so valuable is the open, honest dialogues it facilitates across organizations about which goals are realistic, which goals are ambitious (or totally out of the question), and the empowerment it provides departments and teams to figure out how to get to the best result.

Now that you know what OKRs are and look like, let's move on to the impact of OKRs—why businesses use them and the value they bring.

How this approach evolved from *Measure What Matters*

You might have seen or heard about a different structure in other OKR literature (including John Doerr's *Measure What Matters*). That model is slightly different from the one we just saw and it works like this:

Objective: What you want to achieve

Key Result: What needs to happen to achieve the objective

What does this look like in practice? A key result of a higher-level objective simply becomes the objective for the

---

(*continued*)

next level in the organization. I started with this model, but in using OKRs myself for over 10 years and in working with thousands of customers, I have noticed that the concepts behind the model can be misapplied. This happens in a few fundamental ways:

Because this model combines key results (the outcomes) and key initiatives (the output) into a single key results concept, I have found that organizations end up *using progress on projects as key results*. Doing this does not help shift the organizational mindset from activity to impact.

On the other end of the spectrum, key results are used well to capture outcomes and metrics, but the *execution plan* for reaching the outcomes—what to focus on and what not to focus on—is not clear and execution can get muddled. Capturing key initiatives as part of the objective but separate from key results helps create a holistic picture of the objective so you are able to track progress better.

In John Doerr's perspective, the key result of the higher-level objective automatically becomes the objective for the next level in the organization. This has been misinterpreted to mean that alignment has to be very rigid and everything must cascade from the top. This often results in less-than-inspiring objectives (like getting an average punt return of 25 yards).

Why do we use OKRs to begin with? To provide purpose (the "why") and focus on your organization's top priorities for teams—and balance this with room for ideas from across the organization so that all work *isn't* cascaded from the top, but all work *is* still aligned to the strategic priorities of your business.

To avoid these misunderstandings, I recommend using the model I have outlined, including key initiatives and a collaborative approach to the OKR-setting process. Our view of the OKR framework is not rigid. It's build on flexibility. That's why it has worked in so many different types of organizations. Even if you are not including key initiatives in your structure, as I have recommended, you can still be successful with OKRs in your organization, in fact, our product is even built to be flexible. This book will show you how you can be successful with OKRs, by giving you best practices and the tools to develop the muscle.

2

Why OKRs?

OKRs have proven to be one of the most effective ways to align outcomes, create transparency, and motivate employees to achieve breakthrough productivity.

In *The 2021 State of Goal Management*, our survey of 4,500 US and UK working professionals, we found that those using OKRs do a number of things better than their counterparts who either manage goals using a different framework or use no goal management framework at all.[1]

OKR users indicate that:

- They feel empowered to take risks more frequently than users of other goal frameworks.

---

[1] "State of Goal Management," Ally, https://ally.io/resources/state-of-goal-management/.

- They are more inspired by their work.
- They rate company culture higher than users of other goal frameworks do.

These benefits are more necessary now than ever before. A recent study by McKinsey found that the average lifespan of companies listed in the Standard & Poor's 500 index was 61 years in 1958.[2]

Today, in 2022, it is less than 18 years. McKinsey believes that, by 2027, 75% of the companies currently quoted on the S&P 500 will have disappeared.[3]

Why? Some reasons are business uncertainties, including technology-driven disruptions, global upheavals like COVID-19, mergers and acquisitions, and, perhaps most significantly, the challenge of staying agile to face all these situations as your company grows.

The problem is, as companies grow, increased complexities and inefficiencies lead to greater vulnerabilities and risk. As Emeritus Professor Stéphane Garelli of IMD Business School puts it, "The larger the company, the more energy it needs . . . to survive. In short, large companies spend more time managing themselves than they do managing their clients."[4]

And it's not just large companies that are feeling the heat. The growing pains of countless disruptions and ever-evolving

---

[2]Quoted in Stéphane Garelli, "Why You Will Probably Live Longer Than Most Big Companies," IMD, December 2016, https://www.imd.org/research-knowledge/articles/why-you-will-probably-live-longer-than-most-big-companies/#:~:text=McKinsey%20believes%20that%2C%20in%202027,to%20escape%20this%20mass%20destruction.
[3]Philipp Hillenbrand, Dieter Kiewell, Rory Miller-Cheevers, Ivan Ostojic, and Gisa Springer, "Traditional Company, New Businesses: The Pairing That Can Ensure an Incumbent's Survival," McKinsey & Company, June 29, https://www.mckinsey.com/~/media/McKinsey/Industries/Electric%20Power%20and%20Natural%20Gas/Our%20Insights/Traditional%20company%20new%20businesses%20The%20pairing%20that%20can%20ensure%20an%20incumbents%20survival/Traditional-company-new-businesses-VF.ashx.
[4]Garelli, "Why You Will Probably Live Longer Than Most Big Companies."

market shifts create a pressure-filled dynamic for companies of just about any size.

There are six common challenges I have seen as most prominent in my 30 years in business, and as a leader who works with numerous leaders focused on improving their businesses:

1. **Lack of Alignment:** The work teams are doing isn't connected to the business's topline goals, and derpartments are siloed and focused on disparate activity, creating blind spots, bottlenecks, and duplicate work.

2. **Low agility:** A lack of clear and meaningful measures of success lead to an inability to react quickly when unexpected events come up.

3. **Focus on output:** Many employees find that they're being assessed based on the volume of work they're doing, and the number of deliverables they create; not the value those deliverables add to the business's most important objectives.

4. **Poor visibility:** Leaders aren't able to clearly assess the health of the business, because performance data and progress to core priorities is not available. Likewise, employees don't have a clear line-of-sight into how their work is connected to those priorities.

5. **A low bar:** Often, goals are established to set the bar an employee needs to clear in order to either avoid punative action or gain reward. This doesn't motivate or facilitate a growth mindset.

6. **Infrequent checkins and sporadic process:** Without a formalized process for checkins and updates, each department operates under different parameters, which creates inconsistencies and a lack of accountability.

To solve this problem, countless teams have turned to OKRs as a way to focus, align, and bring clarity on outcomes to ensure that everyone in the company is working together to achieve common goals. It helps to have a solid framework and process you can rely on, as the winds of change inevitably shift around you and your organization.

Massive global enterprise companies have adopted OKRs, and so have 10-person companies. OKRs give companies of any size a strategic advantage for many reasons, and can be adopted by individuals in any role:

1. **OKRs shift focus from output to impact.** By starting with OKRs at the center of business planning, the focus inherently shifts from the outputs your team delivers to the impact they make on the business. In addition to reducing burnout from a lack of clarity around the purpose of that work, this shift in focus helps move the business forward more effectively.

2. **OKRs create cross-functional cooperation to unify direction and improve collaboration.** When each individual, team, and department goal is aligned to the company's broader strategy, teams have a lens through which their work, and the impact it's intended to have, is prioritized.

3. **OKRs help organizations navigate rapid change and reduce risk.** This has been a key benefit of OKRs as companies square off against the pressures COVID-19 brought with it. The OKR framework gives a level of visibility into where efforts are focused, allowing leaders to proactively manage risk, identifying themes and changes in diverse data sets that might have gone unnoticed without a unifying system. This, in turn, helps companies shift focus from activity and output to outcomes, making the right changes at the right time to stay competitive.

In fact, according to our *2021 State of Goal Management Report*, 81% of people using an OKR system say they evaluate and readjust their goals monthly, while only 53% of non-OKR users do.

4. **OKRs create clarity that is documented, measurable, and owned.** With the OKR framework comes accountability that is tracked and measured in the OKR software or document that a company manages the process with. This accountability works two ways: with each individual responsible for their OKRs, and the company leadership responsible for enabling their pursuit.

5. **OKRs inspire stretch and foster involvement.** When done well and made the driving force in a company's strategic rhythm, OKRs can keep every single employee connected to the broader mission and make sure they're invested in their own contribution to it.

6. **OKRs offer clear, contextual communication with continual progress reviews.** The OKR framework doesn't stop when your goals are written. On the contrary, it's designed to create a business rhythm around the most important outcomes that your company is pursuing. It should influence every interaction and drive a review process that pushes for continuous improvement.

Let's dig a little deeper into the specific benefits of OKRs in today's business climate.

Using OKRs to Solve Modern Business Challenges

OKRs are where your mission and values, strategic priorities, and your people come together. They are the rallying point for bringing these three key components of a successful business together, and the glue which holds them together, too.

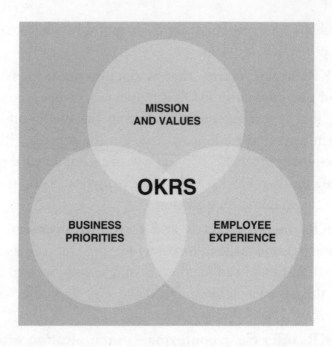

Can you think of a business that would not do well with positive employee engagement, enhanced business performance, and an organizational culture clearly driven by mission and values, all happening simultaneously?

OKRs are the engine that make these dreams a reality, working for and with one another rather than against one another.

For instance, you don't need to choose either rapid business growth or an engaged, happy team. One component feeds the other, and for long-term success, you will need both to run the business.

How many times have we seen a rapidly growing business that can't keep employees in seats and is siloed to within an inch of its life? Or a business that has productive, engaged employees—who all just happen to be working on the wrong things?

OKRs can help solve for all three of these modern business challenges.

The Importance of Visibility and Alignment

Visibility and alignment, a challenge for companies big and small in the best of times, are exacerbated in the hybrid work model accelerated by COVID-19 and other global shifts.

With remote work, there are fewer chances to ask employees, "Hey, how are you?" and then pick up on important cues as they respond. But the data is clear: our people are struggling. And we need to find new ways to help them.

—Jared Spataro, CVP at Microsoft 365[5]

Building an organization where visibility and alignment are part of your lifeblood helps both your employees and your bottom line, because productivity, satisfaction, and clear line-of-sight into outcomes become a lot easier when your employees know where their efforts are pointed—and why.

Real-World Example

How OKRs create visibility and alignment

Patrick is a data manager in the finance department for one of the world's largest independent bottlers.

Patrick describes seeing nearly a 300% increase in productivity from his teams since they implemented a true OKR system. The company had used OKRs in the past,

---

(continued)

---

[5]"The Next Great Disruption Is Hybrid Work—Are We Ready?" from Microsoft Work Trend Index, March 22, 2021, https://www.microsoft.com/en-us/worklab/work-trend-index/hybrid-work.

setting three to five objectives per employee for a year. "Some people could finish all of their objectives in a month or less and then there was no real conversation after that to continue to develop the employee or balance their work. My biggest hindsight realization is 'wow, we really weren't getting as much done as we could've.'"

Today, Patrick and his leadership team spend the last week of each quarter reviewing the previous quarter's objectives and creating new objectives for each group and team member. They talk about high-level objectives and the subsequent individual OKRs. The objectives are a split of 60% core competency training and department initiatives, and 40% directed toward professional development.

It's these professional development objectives that employees in this department would be able to easily push down the road due to the nature of their day-to-day work, but having it as an objective makes it very real. "If you make it somebody's objective, it gets done." The projects can run from data cleanup to huge data migrations that are essential to a growing business.

These meetings also ensure that nothing slips through the cracks.

"If someone does not have an objective nested under one of our CFO's key results, then that helps us analyze who can take the project and plug the holes. We cover all of our bases during this initial meeting to make sure that every initiative is covered."

When every employee can see what everyone else is doing, and that transparency becomes part of the goal-planning process, confidence builds. Each employee can clearly understand the impact their work has on the

> short- and long-term objectives and how their unique position brings value to the success of the company.
>
> This modern approach to widespread transparency and alignment is the key to breaking down company walls and conventional silos that develop between teams and is something that any of us can begin practicing today.

Accelerate Business Growth

Businesses are struggling to improve execution velocity. Do you feel like . . .

- You have no window to quickly know if your business or team is on track to reach its objectives?
- Your goals are siloed and your teams aren't working toward common objectives?
- Your execution is muddled due to a lack of connection between top-level priorities and team or individual goals?
- You lack the tools and cadence for frequent assessment and adjustment at every level of the business?

OKRs keep business priorities and what your team is working on inextricably connected, enabling easy check-ins and a laser focus on outcomes.

- **Create strong alignment between company and team OKRs in your organization.** To achieve your business goals at speed, an obsessive focus around metrics that move the needle can't just be a leadership focus—it needs to become central to your organizational culture. OKRs provide line-of-sight into those metrics and what success looks like for your entire team, so everyone is pointed in the same direction and understands how they are contributing.

The ideal state here is that when things go well, you are intentional about celebrating the wins and how employees have contributed. When you don't see the business outcomes you were looking for, you have a system and set of rituals so that everyone understands what didn't work, what's changing, and why.

- **Increase speed in decision-making and execution.** OKRs help your business increase speed in decision-making and execution by bringing relentless focus to your team and allowing leaders to focus on outcome, not process. This helps businesses get to the "why" more quickly when strong progress is being made toward goals, and when it's not.

  The ideal state here is that every team member feels empowered to make the right decisions on their own and execute at speed, because they are clear on their goals and understand their priorities.

- **Build a growth mindset.** Business as usual doesn't create the kind of momentum that you are looking for. OKRs give you the ability to frame conversations and resource allotment through the lens of impact, not politics. This fosters a culture of innovation.

  The ideal state here is that every team member feels focused on their work and empowered to ask the questions "What's the impact?" and "How does this relate to our OKRs?" on a regular basis.

Real-World Example

How OKRs fuel business growth

In 2019, Adam Boyle had what felt like an impossible task. As VP of Hybrid Cloud Security at Trend Micro, he had to not just maintain his solution's leading market share, he had to simultaneously develop a new platform that included several product units and, in turn, a more continuous set of security services for customers. The new cross-department cloud platform, Trend Micro Cloud One, was poised to be a big initiative for the company—and it had to be launched by year's end.

"We needed an effective, scalable way to get organizational alignment because we had to deliver this thing by the end of the year," Adam says. "I think the company thought it was impossible for us to deliver this on time. We were given a pretty impossible target, but we did it."

OKRs helped Adam and his team make the brand-new security platform with six cloud security services generally available nearly one month before the original plan. "This opened the door to platform-level selling and we closed additional business as a result," he says. "There were an extra 29 days our sales team used to drive leads and close deals."

In the long term, Adam believes OKRs are setting Trend Micro and the Hybrid Cloud Security team up for long-term success and innovative thinking.

Teams from across the globe also are now empowered to work toward a common vision and goal. OKRs have also helped Adam create a culture in which team members feel safe enough to fail. "This psychological safety plays a huge role in shaping our culture and fueling innovation."

- **Increase employee engagement.** Employee burnout. Employee churn. The Great Resignation. What do all of these phenomena have in common? An unhealthy work culture driven by lack of clear purpose and prioritization. A team with focus, a growth mindset, and a sense of trust in their organization and leaders is more engaged and productive. These qualities are fostered by the OKR framework.

- **Increase team focus.** Focus is a prerequisite to increased employee engagement. From *The One Thing* by Gary W. Keller to *Essentialism: The Disciplined Pursuit of Less* by Greg McKeown and the latest in business research, we're learning that we need focus in both our personal and professional lives to do great things. For focus, you need desiloization and alignment, from the beginning of the goal-setting process and on an ongoing basis. OKRs enable this by putting everyone on the same page, enabling goal-setting collaboration and visibility across your organization.

  The ideal state here is that every employee in your organization understands what they are working on and why. Over time and after multiple iterations and retrofits, workload is manageable and no one is biting off more than they can chew. If priorities shift mid-year or -quarter, employees understand how this impacts their everyday work—that is, what work gets removed to accommodate their revised OKRs—and how they will contribute to this new direction.

- **Foster the growth mindset.** Companies need to cultivate a growth mindset (the belief that talents can be developed through hard work, good strategies, and input from others) across the business, and a habitual rhythm of learning and experimentation. The OKR methodology delivers this by encouraging ambitious goal-setting, accountability, and, when things don't work out, a clear sense of what went sideways and where your team needs to shift moving forward.

The ideal state here is that employees feel motivated and inspired at the beginning of each goal-setting period, and feel a balance between work that excites them and could have big impact for the business, and the work that needs to be done to keep the wheels of the business running smoothly.

- **Build a culture of trust.** Employers need to develop a sense of trust for their team members so that autonomous and asynchronous work can be successful. The OKR methodology helps facilitate this by setting clear expectations, ensuring a predictable cadence of meetings and check-ins, and rolling out goals to your company transparently and consistently, so no one feels left in the dark.

The ideal state here is that employees feel connected to their OKRs at all times, understand how they're mapping toward these expectations, and feel comfortable and supported surfacing issues along the way so there are no surprises at the end of the quarter or year.

Real-World Example

Using OKRs to drive employee engagement

Joe Iantosca is VP of Financial Planning and Analysis for Bettercloud, a SaaS management software platform. Before turning to OKRs, Joe describes a decent approach to goal setting, but the context of why was missing for too many employees.

(continued)

"In a lot of ways we had all the pieces there," said Iantosca, speaking of the company's data-driven approach to goal setting prior to adopting OKRs. "But what we needed was some unifying fabric—for everyone in the company to understand how their objectives ladder into what the organization is trying to do."

OKRs incorporate top-to-bottom company involvement and commitment, making every employee a critical piece of the puzzle. This creates buy-in, accountability, and a sense of camaraderie that is necessary for hypergrowth.

3

The History and Evolution of OKRs

OKRs are a 52-year-old methodology, with roots that are almost 70 years old. Yet, while researching this book, our *2021 State of Goal Management* report found that only 29% of US employees even know what OKRs are.[1] This fits with my experience of serving thousands of customers with OKR software over the last few years.

The goal-setting methodology was introduced by long-time Intel CEO Andy Grove and later popularized by John Doerr in his strategic planning masterpiece *Measure What Matters: How Google, Bono, and the Gates Foundation Rock the World with OKRs,* which introduced OKRs to the world stage.[2]

---

[1] "State of Goal Management," Ally, https://ally.io/resources/state-of-goal-management/.
[2] John Doerr, *Measure What Matters: How Google, Bono, and the Gates Foundation Rock the World with OKRs* (New York: Portfolio/Penguin, 2018), https://www.whatmatters.com/the-book.

During his time at Intel, future venture capitalist and author John Doerr was introduced to OKRs by Andy Grove himself. His experience with the framework encouraged him to share it with the founders of Google. According to Doerr's book, the company would go on to 10x the business using OKRs in its planning process—and many other companies would soon follow suit.

OKRs: A Timeline

Modern goal management hit the stage in 1954 with the publication of Peter Drucker's book *The Practice of Management*, where he popularized his management theory known as management by objectives (MBO).

Management by objectives revolutionized performance management and gained popularity, inspiring business managers and leaders at companies such as HP and Xerox (leaders who later attributed their success to the adoption of Drucker's framework).

MBOs enabled organizations to review organizational objectives together, set employee objectives, monitor progress of the work being done to hit those objectives, evaluate results, and give rewards.

While MBOs were effective, they tied employee performance directly with financial rewards, which leads to more conservative goals, a focus on the individual instead of the organization, and a lack of transparency across teams.

Mismanaging performance and rewards can lead to distorted results. If an employee knows they'll receive a bonus for achieving their objectives, they are more likely to set conservative targets than ambitious goals.

The need to decouple performance from financial rewards was something Andy Grove identified several years later at Intel. During his time there (between 1968 and 1997), he implemented,

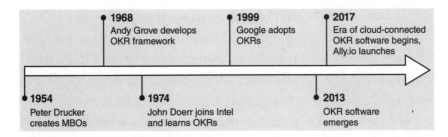

FIGURE 3.1   A simple history of OKRs.

tested, and improved upon Drucker's MBO philosophy which later came to be known as the OKR framework.

Grove's high-output management style not only separated objectives from individual rewards, but introduced key results as the metrics needed to measure impact and contribution. This was the framework he used to successfully transform Intel into one of the world's largest manufacturers of semiconductors.

As you can see in Figure 3.1, the OKR methodology has been around for over 50 years, and in that time, it has drastically evolved. Following is a brief overview of the three distinct phases OKRs have gone through in the past 40-plus years.

OKR 1.0 "The Manual Era"

As Intel Alumni Association president Howard Jacob and board member James Cape told my team recently, "We did this in transparency foils with projectors in the early days. It was cumbersome, but you have to start somewhere. It definitely made the OKR concept of 'transparency' more tangible."

Many companies in the early days of OKRs did things this way, whether with a projector or on paper. This led to excessive turnaround times for reviews and refinement in order for a company to align OKRs across departments. It also drove inefficiencies because each team ran their process differently and true transparency wasn't feasible.

OKR 2.0 "OKR Software V1"

The first generation of OKR software helped bring OKRs into one place for organizations and drive transparency at speed and compile data in a way that hadn't been done before.

These solutions retained the same quality of manual OKR management, with siloed systems, and the feeling of "yet another tool in the enterprise to manage." This clunkiness meant that OKRs failed to take off more broadly as organizations struggled to implement them, and OKRs never became a part of the organization's workflow from top to bottom.

Since they weren't connected to many other systems an enterprise business uses, objectives had to be manually updated. That and the fact that these software solutions weren't embedded in the workflow of users gave this first swathe of systems the feel of "yet another tool" and reduced impact and adoption.

These solutions had the right goal in mind, but not the right feature set to make OKRs for all a reality.

OKR 3.0 "Era of Connected Software"

Over the past few years, companies have turned to the cloud to solve just about every problem, and OKRs are no different. Software solutions have made the OKR framework accessible to everyone through seamless connectivity to data sets and project management tools that propel daily work, and intuitive and simple UX.

In this era of OKR software, there's a short initial learning curve. Iteration, review, and insights into progress happen in real time.

OKR software also connects a company's strategy and goals directly to the tools they use every day via robust integrations, making progress updates instantaneous and accurate, communication and collaboration simple, and transparency in the moment for any employee who needs to understand and contextualize the "why" behind their work and the work being done across the company, as well as the owners, stakeholders, and dependencies for key initiatives.

Regardless of your goal method, it takes a cultural change to roll out a process as integrated and cross-functional as OKRs. This book details that process, but commitment, training, and a growth mindset are necessary to experience the benefits of OKRs.

The Future of OKRs

In the next phase, OKRs will be seamlessly integrated into employee experience, projects, sprints, and individual work. From a glance at their dashboard when they sign on in the morning, employees will understand what they have to do that day, how it ladders up to the objectives, key results, and even mission of their organization, what their work looks like for the rest of the quarter, and have access to tools for enabling productivity, happiness, and health. All in one place, in an intuitive and simple interface.

First, this will occur at only the most successful and sophisticated organizations, but access to increasingly integrated and automated software options will begin to make this employee experience ubiquitous.

In the next decade or so, the assurance that every employee, from leadership to team managers to individual contributors, understands what they're doing, why it matters, and what success looks like will begin to feel like table stakes.

4

OKR Misconceptions, Mistakes, and Myths

In this chapter, I share some of the biggest misconceptions about OKRs—ones you've probably heard or wondered about yourself.

While OKRs have been in use for many years now, adoption has increased rapidly in the last few years, uncovering several outdated ideas about the framework, even as OKRs have evolved to be a much more streamlined and accessible goal management framework. I'd like to clear these up for you.

OKRs Are Only About Measurement

Often, organizations write objectives and key results and do not connect them to key initiatives and projects that need to happen to realize these outcomes. This results in two problems:

1. **There is no real plan to reach these outcomes, and those OKRs become more of a wish list.** The key results of an objective should be a stretch, but realistic, and include the executional plan to realize that objective.

2. **There is no clear way to connect all the key initiatives and projects back to why they are happening in the first place—to the objectives.** Key initiatives and projects drift off course, and often do not have the intended impact in moving the needle on the outcomes. When the need to change an objective arises, these key initiatives and projects do not change with it, making agility nearly impossible.

3. There is no clear context that shows the full picture of an OKR. Not only do we need to see the measures of success, we need to see the activities, side-by-side.

The key initiatives are an integral part of an objective and should be captured as such and tracked. We discuss this more in Chapter 7.

OKRs Are Only for Leadership

Very often the clarity on goals as perceived by leadership disappears when you go down just one or two levels in the organization. It is the team members who sit farther away from the top of the organization who are less sure about why they are doing what they are doing and need clarity and alignment to the top objectives of the organization.

To be effective in getting the entire organization focused on strategic priorities where every team and employee understands and is aligned and engaged in the company's mission and goals, it is important to involve the whole organization in OKRs.

During the rollout of OKRs, when the organization is becoming familiar with them, to manage the change it is a good idea to start from the top of the organization. But even in those early stages, everyone should have visibility into these top-level OKRs, even though they are not writing or owning OKRs.

This helps drive transparency and gets the organization more familiar with OKRs. As the organizations become increasingly adept at using OKRs to drive business, they should methodically roll out OKRs to the next levels—to departments, teams, and, eventually, individuals.

I go into more depth on this in Part IV of this book.

Common Misconception: OKRs Can Be Used Directly to Assess an Individual's Performance

Early in the adoption of OKRs in your organization, I recommend keeping them at the business and team levels to ensure a focus on business performance, rather than individual success, but with the intention that individuals should also eventually have a clear understanding of their objectives (we discuss this further in Part IV when we go through how to roll out OKRs in detail).

A common confusion that stops organizations from adopting OKRs at the individual level is not knowing how OKRs relate to performance at the individual level and other HR processes like talent management and rewards.

While OKRs may initially seem like individual performance management goals for the team manager or individual, the principles behind OKRs and individual performance reviews are vastly different.

OKR Principles	Individual Performance Principles
Stretch: OKRs drive higher business performance by setting stretch goals. Reaching 70–80% of outcomes is deemed a success.	Reviews are designed around realistic expectations. Employees are accountable for delivering 100%, in most cases.
Focus: OKRs focus on three to five key areas to impact the organization's performance.	Employees receive feedback and are rewarded for *all* their contributions, including work that is not linked to organizational OKRs.
Transparency: OKR progress and performance is assessed objectively and is visible to everyone in the organization.	An individual's performance is usually treated as a private discussion between the individual and their manager.

OKRs are about improving your business performance. When OKRs are set at the organization and team levels, they are not intended to be used to assess individual performance, compensation, or rewards.

However, leaving these two important processes completely disconnected will also create confusion for individuals. In your OKR journey, when you reach the stage of rolling out OKRs for individual OKRs, I recommend that you:

- **Keep OKRs focused on business success, and Performance Management on individual success.** OKRs can become an input for performance management, much like the work being done across other systems is today.

  OKRs should be a conversational component of an employee's review to make sure their focus is on business and team impact, but not directly tied to rewards.

- **Do not use the OKR score as the individual's performance rating on the objective.** Maybe the individual took on a very tough objective and still performed admirably, creating learnings that will increase the organization's understanding and shape future success. You do not want to de-incentivize employees from setting stretch goals and trying new things that could positively impact business performance and their own professional growth—this is the opposite of what we're hoping OKRs can achieve. In the performance appraisal context, consider all the factors that impacted the outcome of the OKR, and then decide. It is not uncommon for an objective score to be 0.5, with individual performance rated as excellent.

The bottom line here? Take a balanced approach between OKRs and performance management. Connecting OKRs too tightly to the performance appraisal process dilutes the value of both OKRs and the performance review process, but OKRs should be a key input in performance conversations as employees stretch themselves and tie their everyday activities to business impact.

OKR Is a Rigid, All or Nothing Methodology

OKRs do not have to be inflexible. You can tailor them to suit the unique needs of your organization, and this book will show you how. The following are two specific ways in which there is flexibility within the OKR process.

Committed versus Aspirational

Committed OKRs are goals you are committed to hitting. Aspirational OKRs are goals that you know are stretching the limits of your capabilities and that you may not hit, but that get you and your team to achieve more than what you thought possible.

You can use a mix of committed and aspirational OKRs, or focus on only one type of OKR. You can even have a committed and a stretch target for each key result. The bottom line is that you can choose your own adventure here, and allow your team this flexibility, too.

Tight versus Loose Alignment

There are several options for how you align OKRs in your organization between levels of the business. In *Measure What Matters*, John Doerr focuses on tight alignment, where a company-wide key result becomes the objective for the next level down. In this option, as I mentioned earlier in this chapter, you do not use key initiatives, often risking confusion between your desired measures of success (your key results) and how you get to your objective (your key initiatives).

Options I have seen work more effectively in practice, when we roll in key initiatives, include:

1. **Passing down objectives, key results, and key initiatives from the company level (the highest level in your organization).** The key initiative becomes the objective for the next level down, and this process continues onward through the organization. When a key initiative becomes an objective, the owner of the objective can modify the wording if they feel it's necessary.

2. **Passing down objectives and key results—not key initiatives—from the company level (the highest level in your organization).** Departments then come up with their own objectives, key results, and key initiatives to achieve company objectives and key results, and this process continues onward through the organization.

3. **OKRs are not passed down, and teams create their own.** A department or team identifies which company objectives or key results they can contribute to and then add their

OKRs to achieve them. This option is attractive for companies that focus primarily on alignment to purpose and less on connecting progress.

The most important note here is that this is a collaborative process in which neither company-wide nor department-wide nor team-level nor individual-level OKRs should be written on islands.

The fundamental difference between option 1 and option 2 of this list is that in option 1, the first draft of the company's key initiative, which becomes the objective for the department, was written by the CEO. Then it is edited by the department's objective owner. For option 2, the company's key initiative is drafted by the department that will own it, agreed upon by the CEO, and then it becomes the objective of that department.

There is no one-size-fits-all approach to OKRs, but they should always be part of a collaborative dialogue between leaders, departments, teams, and individual contributors—and this book will give you the best practices you need to choose the right approach for your organization.

OKRs Work Only for High-Tech or High-Growth Organizations

This is one of the most common misconceptions I hear. It is understandable, as the most famous examples we hear about companies successfully using OKRs to drive business outcomes and employee engagement are high-tech companies like Intel and Google.

However, my team and I have enabled over 1,000 teams and business leaders to adopt OKRs and seen successful results across the board, from small to medium-sized businesses to large enterprise companies that are not high-tech or high-growth.

OKRs Are a System of Control for Teams

Sometimes OKRs are perceived as just another way for leaders to assert control over when every team and individual in the organization is working on. OKRs exist to provide context and empower teams and individuals to figure out the right decision in any circumstance based on their close knowledge of your mission and vision, your culture and values, your strategy, and your company-wide OKRs.

The key in avoiding this perception from the get-go is involving your teams when ideating and setting up OKRs, and building the regular communication mechanisms that will not only surface the value in this alignment, but engage your team by asking for recommendations and input.

I also recommend that leaders encourage and spend time understanding the OKRs that are coming from the bottom up. I have seen organizations having two to three objectives cascade from the top, and two to three come from the team level. Sometimes ideas coming from the team get elevated to the department or organizational priority, too.

One more thing: Frequest OKR check-ins are not for keeping tabs on your team, but for helping teams stay focused on top priorities and avoid distractions.

OKRs and KPIs Are Interchangeable

Lets say I'm driving from Seattle to Portland to visit a friend. My objective is to arrive in Portland by a certain time. My key results could be to maintain an average speed of 60MPH, or even to reach specific milestones by specific times. My KPIs, on the other hand, can be everything from my car's tire pressure to the oil life or windshield wiper fluid level. These are important, holistically, but not critical metrics for achieving my objective right now.

KPIs and OKRs complement each other. KPIs cover the breadth of the business and focus on keeping the lights on. There will likely be a lot of KPIs at each level of your business.

OKRs focus on improving a small number of things to increase business performance—placing your bets on what you really think will move the needle. KPIs related to those improvements will often be the KRs for those objectives.

For example, your IT team might have KPIs around your website, tracking things like the site's reliability, how quickly it loads, the number of visits to it per day, and error rate. The IT team will likely have many more KPIs in other areas like resolving service requests in a timely manner, keeping spend under budget, and more.

- Website load time is under 2 seconds.
- Error rate is under .005% of traffic.
- Increase visitors from new region from 2 to 5 million.
- 100% of service requests are responded to in under 24 hours.
- Total spend for website does not exceed $350,000.

Unless these areas need focused improvement to help with the strategic priorities of the business, they will not be the OKRs of the IT department.

The IT department's OKR may be focused on increasing website visits, by standing up a new site for a new geography. The KPI they have around visitors from this region will be one of the key results of the objective, with a target of increasing visitors from 2 million to 5 million. The key initiative of the objective will be "Stand up a new site with regional content by middle of the quarter." The other KPIs, while still valuable to the IT department's other work, are not elevated to the departmental OKRs.

Here's what that looks like:

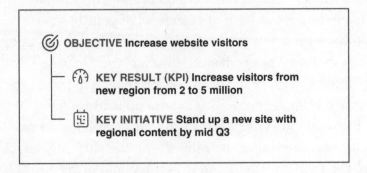

The team will use both KPIs to keep an eye on regular, run-of-the-mill business and OKRs for the areas focused on improvement to support the strategic priorities.

Applying OKR Principles

In Part I, I shared core OKR principles and how OKRs accelerate business results by connecting strategy, execution, and people.

In Part II, we delve deeper into how you can use OKRs effectively, with explanations and examples designed to help your team put OKRs into practice.

OKRs help to create an operating agreement to align the work done across your entire business. You are defining the blueprint for how each department, team, and individual will align to reach the organization's overall business objectives. To achieve this powerful outcome, it requires a thoughtful approach, which I'll lay out in this section.

In the first chapter, we start with a deeper dive into how you should think about crafting your objectives, walking through how to think about objectives in terms of impact, the different types of objectives you should consider for your team or business, and some real-world examples.

In the following chapter, we delve into key results, exploring some of the different types of outcomes, examples, and I'll also share with you an exercise for validating whether you have the right key results for every objective.

Then we get granular about key initiatives and projects, with examples of how to connect key initiatives to your objectives.

I share an interactive workshop that you and your team can use to draft your own OKRs, offer practical guidance for OKR rituals including check-ins and retrospectives, and finish with some of the most common OKR questions I see from leaders like yourself. Finally I'll provide specific guidance on how to use OKRs at different levels of the business: the organizational level, departments like Strategy and Operations, Human Resources, Marketing, Sales, and more, including examples and insight from functional leaders.

5

Defining Your Objectives

The first part of a well-written OKR is the objective statement itself. The "O" in your OKRs, the objective, is a clear, concise, and inspiring statement of what you want to accomplish.

In this chapter, we'll discuss what makes a good objective, and we'll talk about the other two components (key results and key initiatives) in the next two chapters.

When written effectively, your objective statement will connect to your mission, bring focus to the most important business outcomes you need to drive, create clarity across your organization or team, and inspire your team to develop a growth mindset. This focus, clarity, and inspiration shows up in how you write your objectives.

Each objective should be simple, clear, and concise. I generally recommend keeping an objective to one line. An objective should also focus on the impact (the desired business result) you're hoping to achieve, not the activity of your team.

To put this in perspective, think of your objective as the destination on a map, not the waypoints used to navigate to that point. Let's dive into key aspects to think about when writing your objectives.

Make Your Objectives Time-Bound

An objective needs to have a clear timeframe in which it needs to be accomplished. Usually, we see business objectives defined annually *and* quarterly. The annual OKRs provide the long-term context for the quarterly OKRs, which bring more urgency to move the needle every three months. I'll share more about OKR cycles later in the business rhythms section (Part III).

Your objectives do not have to end precisely at the end of your quarterly or annual OKR cycle—the date by which the objective needs to be accomplished can be earlier than the end of the year or quarter.

Start with the "Why"

If you're writing the business's top-level objectives, a helpful exercise is to review your mission, vision, values, and long-term strategic priorities. A good objective connects the organization to that larger purpose. Anything you do decide to focus on over this year or quarter needs to be aligned to the longer-term goals. Without this longer-term picture, your near term (quarterly or biannually), you run the risk that the OKRs may not be well aligned toward the strategic priorities.

When defining objectives for a team or department, you'll want to understand the next-level-up OKRs for the same time period before creating yours, as this will provide the "why." If the long-term or high-level objectives are not available yet, you can still draft your OKRs to make progress, but try to reconcile them later against the higher-level or long-term objectives.

Objectives Should Create Focus

A good set of objectives brings focus to the plans being drawn up by each department, team, or individual in your organization.

Limit defining your objectives to three to five objectives for each level of the organization. The intent is to shine a spotlight on the most critical areas of the business you can impact in a given time period. Your goal is not to shine a floodlight on every status quo activity and KPI across the business.

As you progress deeper throughout an organization, you may find that having fewer OKRs makes a team more productive. It keeps teams locked in on the area of the business—an area you've already determined is critical—on which they can have the most impact. This also keeps an organization from spreading itself too thin.

Objectives Should Inspire

Picture yourself hosting the year-end celebration for all your employees, celebrating the massive success you had this year. The clock is winding down; you address the crowd and summarize what you have achieved for the year. What is the story you tell?

In other words, if you could look back at the end of the year and accomplish only three to five things, which ones would make the most dramatic impact on your business?

Committed and Aspirational Objectives

A common OKR question I hear is "How many of my OKRs should be around hard commitments, and how many should be stretch?"

- **Committed Objectives:** Goals that need to be achieved. Resources and schedules should be adjusted to make sure they get done.
- **Aspirational Objectives:** Ambitious goals designed to stretch the owner or team in order to move the business forward. These goals are not expected to be 100% attained. Rather, 70–80% is considered good.

An aspirational objective is intended to stretch you and your team. It fosters a growth mindset by forcing you to ask, "If this target is higher than what we expect we can do, what will we do differently to reach it?"

This is where the connection of an objective to its key results becomes essential. An aspirational objective needs aspirational measures of success (more on this in the next chapter).

I generally recommend that the vast majority, if not all, of your OKRs be aspirational. Over time, aim for at least three to four of your five objectives to fall into this category.

Your objectives should inspire a growth mindset for everyone in your organization, but they need to add clarity around where you expect your team to grow.

If you're driving toward a 2023 IPO, that becomes a rallying point as much as it is an objective to track. It also provides the context needed for each department to think about what their contribution to that objective is, and how it fits with other departments. This isn't "status quo" work. It's ambitious and will force the team to think outside the box.

Objectives Should Create Balance

In general, you'll want to capture multiple areas with your three to five objectives. This ensures a healthy balance instead of all objectives focusing on one area of the business or team. I have commonly seen the following four areas in the top-level objectives of an organization.

1. **Business Growth:** This first category of objectives is about financial performance like growth and profitability. This category can be a good place to start, since it often fuels the growth of other areas.

2. **Customer:** The second category is focused on customers. This can include satisfaction, retention, engagement, referrals, or adoption. The intent is more important than the metric itself. When it comes to customer experience, what is important to you and your business?

3. **Product or Service:** This third category is around your offering. These are the goals you have for what you sell, whether that's accounting software or yoga clothing, or the service you provide, such as tax preparation or fitness classes. Product or service objectives are often focused on innovation, quality, efficiency, or speed.

4. **People:** This fourth category is around your people. Your internal team of employees is one of your most valuable (and expensive) assets, so use this category to set goals around hiring, retention, employee engagement, or fostering company culture. These categories contextualize the work that needs to be done to realize your mission.

What Does a Good Objective Statement Look Like?

Let's look at two different OKRs. One is well-written, the other is not.

- **Good:** Set our company up for an IPO by next year.
- **Bad:** Continue sales and customer success handoff process to maintain customer experience.

Now, let's identify what makes one good and the other bad.

The Good	The Bad
Short and concise	Long and verbose
Clear why this objective matters for the business	Unclear why this objective is important
Timebound ("by next year")	Not timebound
Inspiring (an IPO is a major accomplishment)	Uninspiring (continued work is status quo, not stretch)

Writing good objectives might be a bit challenging initially, but it does become easier with practice. Making sure that the OKRs you draft will be impactful on every person in your business can be one of the most important planning activities you undertake.

In the next two chapters, we'll expand on these themes with our key results and key initiatives, but at the end of Part II, you'll find many more examples to inspire your own company and departmental objectives.

6

Defining Your Key Results

With an objective having been defined, you'll move into the process of bringing clarity to the outcomes of that objective. What will the measures of success be?

These are the objective's key results, and they measure the outcome of an objective. A key result is meant to drive clarity by establishing what success of that objective actually means.

Key results are a core aspect of shifting focus from activity to impact. In addition to bringing clarity and focus on the outcomes, key results also provide the ability to track progress at regular intervals, so that you know if you're on track, and take any corrective action necessary before it is too late. Last, key results are used to score the objective at the end of your quarterly or annual OKR cycle—they provide an objective way to assess and learn.

Key Results Should Create Clarity

For each objective, you'll want to have three to five key results that add up to successfully achieving that objective. Having three to five key results for an objective is the rule of thumb because it adds the right amount of clarity to that objective. If you have too few key results, you may not be measuring the success in a balanced, holistic way. Having too many key results dilutes the clarity and focus.

In general, your key results should be quantitative, objectively measurable outcomes of impact of achieving the objective.

For example, let's say the objective is to "Earn customer love and trust"; one key result is could be:

Increase NPS (net promoter score) by five points

This clearly captures the impact of the objective, and NPS is objectively measurable throughout the quarter or year through customer surveys and other tools.

Outcomes over Outputs

A common issue I see is that many times, people develop key results based on outputs rather than outcomes. Output-driven key results are task-motivated and largely capture the work that will be done, not the intended impact.

Outcome-driven goals start with the end in mind, not the beginning. If you start with the output, you may know that you're driving, but you don't know your destination. If you start with the outcome or impact, you can work backward to define the right projects and key initiatives.

This seemingly simple shift in how you measure the success of an objective is one of the core benefits of OKRs—to shift your team's focus from work that is being done to the impact of the work toward the team and business objectives.

What Does a Good Key Result Look Like?

Let's look at two different key results. One is well-written; the other is not. In this case, let's say the objective is to "Delight users and improve engagement."

- **Good:** Increase MAU (monthly active users) from 50,000 to 85,000.
- **Bad:** Add new integrations to website product pages and improve navigation to drive conversion of visitors.

Now, let's identify what makes one good and the other bad.

The Good	The Bad
Short and concise	Long and verbose
Focus on impact	Focus on projects and activity
Objectively measurable, through analytics systems	Somewhat vague as it is hard to measure things like "improve navigation"

Writing good key results, just like objectives, becomes easier with practice. Making sure that the OKRs you draft will be impactful on every person in your business can be one of the most important planning activities you undertake.

Sometimes, the impact of an objective may not be measurable within the same quarter or year. I see this often in product development, where the outcome for the time period is to deliver something and the impact of that will be measurable in subsequent time periods. In those cases, planning, preparation, and delivery milestones can be useful as *leading indicators*—key results intended to tell you that you're heading in the right direction—and in the subsequent quarters you would have OKRs that measure the impact of the work. It would be better if the work can be sliced in a way to see an impact within that quarter or year, but where that is not possible, using lead indicators would be practical.

Committed and Aspirational Key Results

Just like your objectives, key results can be either committed or aspirational. Typically, key results of a committed objective will have the expectation that 100% of the targets will be achieved.

An aspirational key result is an outcome that falls outside either historical norms or what the owner would otherwise commit to reaching. Attaining 70–80% of the targets is considered good.

It is okay to blend committed key results with aspirational ones. Determining the type should be reliant on whether the objective is considered committed or aspirational.

The Process of Defining Key Results

Here is an example of how defining key results can work in practice.

Meet Susan. Susan is the CEO of a software company. Susan and her team set a company objective:

"Achieve record revenue growth."

Before digging into specifics, Susan and her team step back and think about their challenge at a high level. What does "record revenue growth" mean? If the revenue growth the previous year was 25% and the organization reached $100 million, maybe this year they aspire to 30% growth. The key result might be:

Key Result: Drive revenue growth of 30%.

Alternatively, Susan and her team could be more explicit, expressing that revenue growth as a dollar figure to keep the team focused on a target:

Key Result: Drive $130 million in revenue.

Some organizations might have several types of revenue: recurring revenue, billed revenue, or even product versus service revenue. These specifics can be added as well to bring clarity, or this can be left to departments to establish at the next level. This key result could simply add that context, and look something like this:

Key Result: $130 million in billed revenue.

This key result has brought clarity to what it means to achieve record revenue growth. It enables the organization to see progress over time and take corrective actions where necessary. However, it is somewhat unbalanced. Would the organization want to achieve record growth at *any* cost? If we assume the answer is no, it would be good to add a key result to clarify that and provide guardrails for the organization. Let us say Susan's team wants to improve profit margins as well, from 13% last year to 15% this year. They would add another key result to the objective:

Key Result: Increase profit margin to 15%.

This is also an objectively measurable outcome. Revenue and profitability metrics are most likely tracked in the financial systems or spreadsheets from the finance team. OKR software solutions can connect with financial or business intelligence systems to automatically update the key results to provide visibility into progress of the OKR and provide visibility into OKR progress status.

Susan and her team may want to create a long-term focus as well, to add even more balance to this revenue target. While the organization is driving toward a revenue goal, they also want to set themselves up for success in the future, which they could do by making sure they are selling to the right customers. That would look something like this:

Key Result: 60% of new customers come from the core enterprise segment.

With those three key results defined, here is what Susan and her team have come up with:

Objective: Achieve record revenue growth.

- **Key Result 1:** Drive $130 million in billed revenue.
- **Key Result 2:** Increase profit margin to 15%.
- **Key Result 3:** 60% of new customers come from the core enterprise segment.

By developing three to five respective key results that will help them accomplish each objective, Susan and her team are able to measure the impact they're making on their highest business priorities.

Perform the Necessary and Sufficient Test

Once the objective and its key results are defined, conduct what is called *the necessary and sufficient test*.

Look at your objective and its key results and ask: "Are all these key results *necessary* to reach our objective?"

If the answer is yes, then they pass the necessary test. If the answer is no, spend more time refining the key results to be more relevant and measurable and to make sure you have a plan of action to achieve your objective.

Repeat the exercise, but this time ask: "If I accomplish all my key results, will I have achieved my objective?"

If the answer is yes, then they pass the sufficient test. If the answer is no, you need to spend more time defining stronger key results.

7

Defining Your Key Initiatives

Remember that OKRs are intended to provide a spotlight on your most critical priorities as a business, not a floodlight on everything the business is doing. This is true of the goals you set, the metrics you track, and the work your team does to reach those goals.

It's important to differentiate day-to-day work that is necessary to keep the lights on from the key initiatives and projects that will move the needle on your core objectives.

What is a key initiative? Think of the work that *needs* to be done in order to achieve an objective. You will apply the "necessary and sufficient" test, which we just walked through for our key results, here as well. Your key initiatives will live alongside the key results that are both necessary and sufficient to achieve our objectives.

A key initiative can be any project at the business or team level. Or it can be delegated to a specific department or functional group, when it becomes an objective for that team, with key results and key initiatives of its own.

Key Initiatives Should Create Context

There are four characteristics to focus on when developing key initiatives.

1. **Resourced:** Your OKRs are timebound, so the work being done to achieve them should reflect your team's ability to reach those objectives. Set realistic and ambitious (but achievable) deadlines for the key initiatives you and your team commit to, and be sure that you have the right resources, investment from stakeholders, time, and dollars allocated.

2. **Focused:** A big mistake many people make when planning work is that they're too ambitious. While you can have numerous key initiatives for every objective, it often works best to pick a handful for any given quarter and execute well on those. Be critical about your and your team's ability to focus an initiative, and question whether you're stretching too thin. OKRs are about focus, but as you start to outline the work you'll do to reach an objective, there is a tendency to lose that focus.

3. **Trackable:** A key initiative needs to be trackable, so you know if you're on track to your objective. These should be simple to contextualize alongside your key results.

4. **Clear:** A key initiative isn't one of a thousand projects on a project board. It's a core priority for the business. It should be clear and easy to understand in short order for any senior leader or staff who needs to understand why it is a priority.

Key Initiatives in Practice

Let's bring back Jane, the CEO of the hypothetical software company with the following goal.

Objective: Achieve record revenue growth

- **Key Result 1:** Drive $130 million in billed revenue.
- **Key Result 2:** Increase profit margin to 15%.
- **Key Result 3:** 60% of new customers come from the core enterprise segment.

To drive $130 million in billed revenue, the company's strategy could be to add $25 million in new customer revenue and grow existing customer revenue from $100 million to $105 million.

To implement this strategy, the key initiatives could be:

- **Key Initiative 1:** Generate $25 million in new customer revenue.

   This key initiative could be cascaded to the sales team and become their objective.

- **Key Initiative 2:** Develop new offerings and upgrade existing customers.

   This could be a business-wide initiative that product, sales, and customer success teams would work on together.

The goal of aligning key initiatives to your objectives is to organize the biggest rocks you need to move for the quarter, not to capture every single task you'll take on for the given time period. Those can still be tracked in the detailed project plans you're used to and distilled in your OKRs for clarity and alignment.

In fact, much of this process can be automated through integrated SaaS products. Connecting project management (either natively or by connecting to your project management software) to OKRs doesn't have to be a chore, and it will make your business clearer to everyone involved, from strategy to execution.

Work, in general, is planned based on ongoing needs and optimizations, and seldom around the big bets. As you set these more ambitious objectives, the work needs to support them. Don't neglect project planning in the context of your OKR cycle.

A successful OKR program encapsulates the key initiatives, projects, and tasks needed to reach that objective. When talking about *how* you achieve your mission, vision, values, and objectives, the projects, campaigns, and tasks you do to reach them are needed. But you'll notice I said "key" initiatives. OKRs are not a task management solution. Remember, this is about providing a spotlight on your biggest bets, not tracking every single thing.

8

Aligning and Cascading Your OKRs

In this chapter, you'll learn how to take the OKRs you've established at a leadership level and cascade them to each department and team. This process can be tricky, but remember to stay flexible. Not every department is built the same, and not every department will neatly fit into each box. This process is collaborative and takes iteration to get right.

There are different ways you can cascade OKRs across your company. Ultimately, you'll pick a structure that makes the most

sense for the objectives you're trying to reach and the people
who will play a part in them.

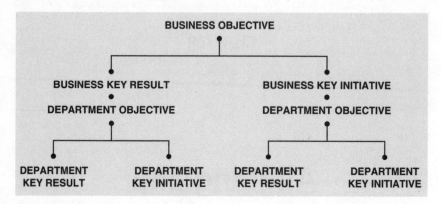

In general, top-level (company) objectives should be outlined first to give the rest of the company direction. Departments and teams need to plan their goals with these topline
business needs in mind, and their goals should align up to the
company OKRs.

I talk more about the process for the planning and meetings involved in Parts III and IV, but in general terms, once the
topline business OKRs are defined, the remaining OKRs for
departments, teams, and individuals can be set to either directly
align to the company level OKRs or, if there is a core outcome a
specific department needs to drive that doesn't fit neatly, to stand
alone. A general rule of thumb that my team recommends is that
80% of OKRs should be aligned to the level above them, but
20% not being aligned is acceptable.

I recommend that you have the same owner for both
the objectives and the key results at every level across your
organization.

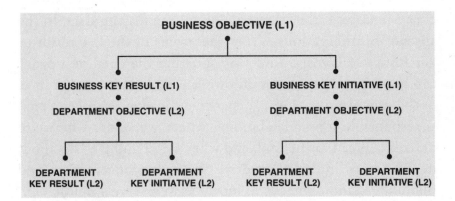

For example, as the CEO of a company, I would own—and am accountable for—all of the business objectives *and* the key results for them. That doesn't mean these are created in a silo and dictated to the company; they are created collaboratively with input from the executive management team, who may in turn involve members of their own teams for input and feedback.

The broader senior leadership team would then take these OKRs back to their departments to create their departmental OKRs. They will align their objectives with the objectives of their CEO. Guidance is for executive leaders to look at which company key results they drive, and which they merely support. This enables them to write their own objectives more effectively and with more clarity. A topline key result might have a different metric from a departmental key result. Both may be critical to the business.

In an ideal state, a software platform is used that is integrated with each system your company uses, with all key results and progress toward key initiatives automatically updated and data driven. This allows owners to focus on adding context via check-in notes rather than spending time finding data. In the absence of integrations, either the owner of the key result or key initiative is responsible for updating the data, or a proxy can be assigned as a check-in owner. The leader for that level of the organization (CEO, department leader, team lead, etc.) is responsible for understanding where we stand, why we're on track, ahead, or behind, and what we're going to do about it. OKRs are intended to drive the right conversation, and that understanding needs to move between levels fluidly.

When writing OKRs, you're making bets across your company as to where the focus should be and what the outcomes you're aiming to achieve are. If you've made the right bets and your company is aligned, you should achieve the higher-level outcomes by achieving the lower-level outcomes. Your time should be spent talking about and analyzing results of your bets (your OKRs) rather than trying to create a tight path of alignment across your organization.

The Right Number of Levels

At a minimum, companies (or suborganizations, if OKRs aren't being used across the company yet) should be establishing OKRs for two levels. This often finds itself taking the form of "Business" (owned by the CEO) and "department" (owned by each departmental leader). You do not necessarily need team- and individual-level OKRs, and if this is your first time using OKRs at your organization, I recommend you don't. In Part IV, I share a phased approach that details this more clearly, but remember that to successfully embed OKRs within your organization, you should think in terms of change management. In order for OKRs to enable every employee, the framework needs to stick for managers and executives.

Now, individuals don't need to *own* OKRs to get value out of them. The company- and department-level OKRs should be visible to all and a part of regular company communication so they are internalized by the entire team. This will also serve to prime the broader organization for eventual full-scale adoption.

Starting with two levels of OKRs ensures collaboration between organizations across your company and ensures that at a high level your different departments are aligned to the company's goals.

If you choose to create OKRs for individuals in your organization, that individual's OKRs need to align to the level above or laterally to another department. Individual OKRs should never align directly to the business-level (L1) objectives, when there are layers between the two. If teams and individuals do not align only to the level above them or laterally to their peers, the alignment exercise will become too complex and too busy to create a clear understanding of which groups are contributing to which big bets.

Choosing Your Cascading Method

As I mentioned earlier, there are two common methods of cascading OKRs.

The first, and more traditional, method of *Measure What Matters* fame is what we'll call "tight alignment." In this scenario, the key results from one level become the objectives for the next level. This tight alignment has received its fair share of praise and criticism, and it has served many successful companies well. However, for the modern, distributed, and often more matrixed organization, this is much more rigid than is appropriate.

For those companies, I recommend what we'll call "loose alignment." With a loose alignment structure, departments and teams have the flexibility to still directly cascade a company key result (or a key initiative) into a new objective, but they can also choose to create a new second-level objective that aligns directly to the company's topline objective. This method has drawn criticism and praise, but, in my experience, the criticism comes from OKR purists who feel a sense of affinity for the tightly aligned structure, whereas practitioners who are focused simply on finding the best solution to their problem are more drawn to this loose approach, which they can tailor to fit their business. In this model, key initiatives can also roll directly up to an objective.

Let's look at an example of each method, and how the alignment works.

Method #1: Tight Alignment

With tight alignment, cascading happens directly. Here's an example of how to cascade OKRs using the tight alignment method, where a company-level key result becomes a department-level objective.

Company Objective: Earn customer love and trust.

Company Key Result: Increase retention rate to 99% in Q4.

Jane (VP, Customer Success) Objective: Increase retention rate to 99% in Q4.

Jane (VP, Customer Success) Key Result: Implement customer improvement plan for 100% of at-risk customers by December.

Jane (VP, Customer Success) Key Result: Increase NPS score from 7 to 8.5 in Q4.

Jane (VP, Customer Success) Key Result: Increase customer engagement from 1x a month to 2x a month by December.

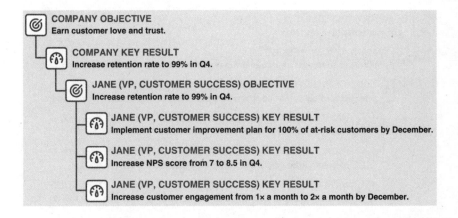

Jane starts by inheriting the key result from the company objective. Her objective has two key results she will use to measure the success of this objective.

Because this objective will require the support of other team members, the key results will cascade to other team members—becoming one of their objectives. "Implement customer improvement plan for 100% of at-risk customers" will now become one of the quarterly objectives for Nick, the director of customer success. Nick will identify three to five key results that will help him measure whether he reached his goal.

Nick (Director of Enterprise Success) Objective: Implement customer improvement plan for 100% of at-risk customers.

Nick (Director of Enterprise Success) Key Result: Reduce customer response time from 72 hours to <24 hours.

Nick (Director of Enterprise Success) Key Result: Increase total amount of completed quarterly business reviews (QBRs) from 88% to 100%.

Nick (Director of Enterprise Success) Key Result: Develop an action plan with three improvements and implement this quarter.

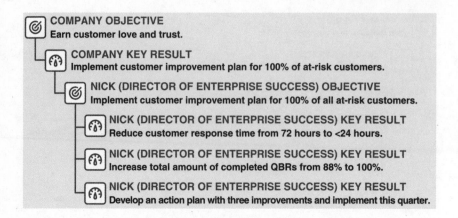

From here, the OKR can continue to cascade until it reaches each independent contributor on Nick's team.

Method #2: Loose Alignment

The other OKR alignment approach is to create business objectives, key results, and key initiatives, and allow each department and team to identify their own OKRs that support the company-wide goal.

Here's how that works in practice:

Jane (VP, Customer Success) Objective: Improve customer satisfaction.

Jane (VP, Customer Success) Key Initiative: Identify top three drivers causing friction and implement corrective action.

Jane (VP, Customer Success) Key Result: Reduce customer response time to <24 hours.

Jane (VP, Customer Success) Key Result: Resolve 90% of open cases.

Jane (VP, Customer Success) Key Initiative: Develop customer advisory board.

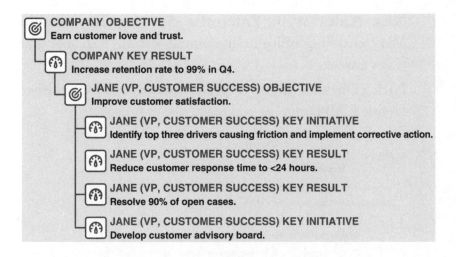

Jane understands the company plans to measure the success of their objective through NPS scores.

Choosing to focus on improving customer satisfaction is an objective that will contribute and impact the company's goal. Much like Jane, Nick must create an OKR that is both relevant and will impact the company's focus on earning customer love and trust.

Nick finds an opportunity to increase the company's customer satisfaction (CSAT) score. To help improve customer satisfaction, Nick decides to focus on implementation. His objective then becomes "increase our customer satisfaction for implementation" and CSAT >4.5 becomes a KR. Some of the work Nick and his team do is focused on the key initiative reflected in Jane's OKRs, and serves the need for a customer advisory board.

Nick (Director of Enterprise Success) Objective: Increase our customer satisfaction for implementation.

Nick (Director of Enterprise Success) Key Initiative: Deploy new onboarding and implementation process.

Nick (Director of Enterprise Success) Key Result: Implement new customer community with 65% engagement rate.

Nick (Director of Enterprise Success) Key Result: Make customer office hour training sessions available four times a week.

Nick (Director of Enterprise Success) Key Initiative: Define CAB target list and reach out to prospects.

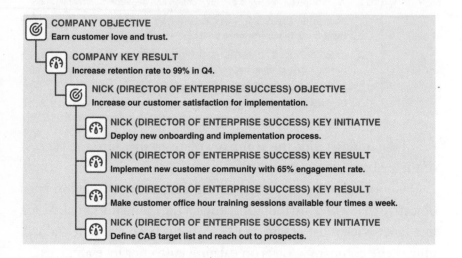

In this example, both Jane and Nick create relevant and measurable key results they can use to discern whether they achieved their goals and key initiatives outlining how they will achieve them.

Aligning Across Departments and Teams

Goals and work are too often disconnected. This is because strategy development happens top-down, but work is planned bottom-up, without a process to connect the two and rectify gaps, creating disconnects in several parts of the chain.

But how do you stop that? How do you bring every employee's work in line with the most important objectives of the company? How do you work bottom-up *and* top-down?

This all boils down to one of the most game-changing aspects of OKRs: alignment.

There are three critical areas of alignment when it comes to initiatives, projects, and tasks:

- Aligning to OKRs
- Aligning within a team or department
- Cross-functional alignment

In this section, we explore these opportunities for cross-company alignment and how they strengthen an OKR program.

Team Alignment

Within a given department or team, aligning around work should happen as part of the planning cycle.

Start with the departmental objectives that are aligned to the company objectives, and from there, set your key results and key initiatives. These KRs and KIs, in turn, give your team direction on the work they should focus on: the projects that will help your team reach the OKRs you've set. This planning takes into consideration bandwidth, time and deadlines, and dependencies. With this detailed outline of both the work that needs to be done and, potentially, that *can't* realistically be done, you reverse course to ensure that the individual key results and objectives and the department key results and objectives are still the right areas of focus and, just as important, are still within reach.

Cross-Functional Alignment

More complex than intradepartmental alignment is interdepartmental alignment. Dependencies and overlap exist between teams that have different OKRs, different areas of focus, and distractions that may not even be on your radar.

For cross-functional planning, I recommend a matrixed approach, repeated with each department to address inconsistencies, overlap, and dependencies, as shown in the following example.

Marketing Objective 1	Marketing Key Results 1	Marketing Key Initiative 1	Marketing IC Task 1
Overlap with product OKRs?	Dependencies on product to achieve this key result?	Dependencies on product to complete project? Overlap?	Dependencies on product stakeholders to complete task?

In this example, the marketing team walks the product team through each of their OKRs and the associated work to determine if there is overlap or dependencies in the plan. The product team repeats the process with marketing, and the conversation concludes with either alignment or the realization that something is missing.

One of the biggest problems I see with planning actual work is that it happens in a silo. Teams don't share the executional plan with other departments, just the high-level strategy, which creates redundancy and missed opportunities.

While it takes time to do this with each department, doing it will set your department up for success.

Expert Spotlight: Rick Klau, "How Google Sets Goals"

You may be one of the 1 million-plus viewers of Rick Klau's YouTube video "How Google Sets Goals: OKRs," but if you're not, a little background: Rick spent more than 13 years at Google, most recently as a senior operating partner for Google Ventures. Before that, he was the VP of publisher services for FeedBurner, acquired by Google. He is now the chief technology innovation officer for the state of California.

Here he shares his expert opinion on what you need to know about OKRs before getting started.

1. **Commit to less but be overambitious.** These qualities made OKRs critical to Google's success.

2. **Leadership buy-in is table stakes.** The top priority should be making sure leadership understands what OKRs are and why they're important—and conveys that to the entire organization.

3. **Engage in the OKR process with a growth mindset.** Don't assume you're going to get OKRs "right" the first time. One of the best things that a CEO can do is demonstrate to her team that no one is getting a scarlet letter because they got a zero on an OKR. No one is getting punished. We've learned something. That informs the next set of predictions we make about the outcomes we can accomplish, or potentially we've learned where there are headwinds that we didn't know about.

4. **Don't worry about individual OKRs (at first).** After conversations with hundreds of startup founders and leadership teams, what I've learned is: don't worry about individual OKRs. Focus on setting a handful of objectives at the company level—the fewer, the better. Companies always tell me they need four or five or six. I always tell them they've only got three, two would even be better, and then translate that from

(continued)

the company level to the team level. Don't go any further at first.

5. **After OKR fluency comes individual OKRs.** OKRs are like learning a language. Once your teams have developed a fluency in how to communicate with each other about what it is you're doing and what you have agreed to not do, you can bring in individual commitments.

6. **Embedding OKRs into your culture creates clarity and speed.** I was part of the team building what became Google+. Sergey was in basically every major strategy meeting for months. At some point his focus shifted, so he wasn't at as many of those meetings, but because OKRs were so ingrained in how the organization operated, we all knew how Larry and Sergey thought about decision-making. When we had decisions to make, it was as if we could channel Larry and Sergey into the room and say, well, if they were here, this is what they would say. You would get to some consensus because you already had that framework that had been communicated the prior quarter and the quarter before that about what was most important and how to measure whether we had the outcome that we wanted.

7. **The most valuable part of OKRs is what's *not* in your OKRs.** The true value of OKRs is what you're giving yourself permission to say no to without the feeling of politics or playing favorites. There is no faster way to kill momentum or initiative at a company than to disincentivize creativity. If you don't have something like OKRs in place that makes it easy and comfortable and apolitical for those "no's" to come, then people start to get frustrated because they don't understand how decisions get made.

9

Writing OKRs: An Interactive Team Workshop

If this is your first pass at writing OKRs with your team, it can feel a bit daunting. Where do you start? How do you organize the work?

This chapter provides an interactive workshop framework meant to help alleviate common challenges and missteps when writing OKRs as a team, by providing step-by-step direction on how to develop meaningful and impactful objectives and the key results that will contribute to the quantitative success of those objectives.

> **TIP:** Setting OKRs requires a bidirectional approach that starts with high-level company objectives (or team objectives distilled from company priorities), then cascades down to the rest of the organization. From there, each employee works with you as their manager, providing input on how to best define their individual OKRs.

Pre-Workshop Checklist

- **Identify the OKR Champion:** Much like a scrum master and owner, it's crucial to identify who will be responsible for leading the initiative in your team. With a smaller team, this might be you. This person will mentor and coach the people on your team, ensuring that everyone is engaged and participates. This person will also be responsible for making sure there is a system in place to track and measure the team's OKRs. I share more on the OKR Champion role in Chapter 22.

- **Team input:** Before beginning the workshop, ask your team to come prepared to share ideas on which objectives and supporting key results they feel the team should focus on in the upcoming months. If company OKRs have been communicated, the team should use those as a baseline for priority.

Workshop Timeline

Brief Overview

Spend the first 30 minutes of the meeting introducing your team to the basic concepts of OKRs. Each person must understand the rhythm, formula, and basic terminology, as well as what OKRs aren't, and how they should plan to score them at the end of the period. Defining this information up front will help set proper expectations of what the team can anticipate during this exercise.

The following section is an outline for you to use as a primer for this section.

Understanding the OKR Formula

Defined as "objectives and key results," OKRs are designed to help you answer two distinct questions:

1. Where do I want to go?
2. How will I know I'm getting there?
3. What will I do to get there?

There is a standard formula for goal setting through OKRs:

Objectives: Qualitative, aspirational goal an individual, team, or company wants to achieve. It is the final result or outcome.

Key results: Measurable, quantitative metrics that contribute to the achievement of an objective. These results show the progress of how close an individual or team is getting to achieving an objective.

Key Initiatives: These are the actions that will be taken to achieve key results.

- **For higher-level objectives like company objectives:** These will likely be objectives cascaded to departments and business units.
- **At the department level:** Initiatives may be the objectives that are cascaded down to individual teams.
- **For team and individual objectives:** Initiatives will likely be projects that will executed to reach the outcomes.

> **TIP:** Make sure you have the ability (the resources and timeline) to complete your initiatives—that's what makes the objective realistically optimistic.

Remember

- **OKRs aren't unrealistic or ambiguous goals.** They should be ambitious, achievable, and well defined, but still push you and your team.
- **OKRs aren't to-do lists.** They should serve a broader purpose that connects monthly and quarterly performance to the overarching business goals and strategy. They should also be shareable across the organization to inspire collaboration, transparency, alignment, and focus.

Step One: Identify the Business Goal, or Strategic Purpose

15 minutes Your objectives are intended to bring greater alignment, clarity, and agility to each and every part of the business. It's important that you and your team understand the company priorities before writing any team or personal OKRs, so start by listing your company priorities. You can do this using a whiteboard or any one of the many virtual collaboration tools out there.

Step Two: Choose How Your OKRs Will Cascade

As I mentioned in Chapter 4, there are two main ways of cascading OKRs to your team: loose and tight alignment. Tight alignment gives greater control to the team creating the topline OKRs, while loose alignment gives more flexibility to department leaders and team managers.

Step Three: Define Your Objectives

For this exercise, start by defining three to five objectives you'd like to tackle. Keep your objectives clear, simple, and inspiring. It can be valuable to frame with a verb to keep the objective actionable, for example, "Make every OKR owner in our company successful." Now start by defining three to five sample objectives you would like to focus on for the upcoming time period.

Step Four: Define Your Key Results

Remember, key results must be measurable and time bound, and will be the measure by which you know if the objective was achieved or not. Don't include more than five key results per objective to ensure your goals are achievable. Develop three to five key results per objective that will tell you that you've accomplished that objective. When possible, use this formula:

Verb + what you're going to measure + from x to y

For example: "Increase attendance from 350 to 500 people."

Step Five: Define Your Key Initiatives

Alongside your key results for each objective, define the three to five key initiatives your team will need to drive in order to achieve this objective. These are the core activities that you want to capture, not every single project.

Step Six: Validate Your OKRs Through the Necessary and Sufficient Test

Look at your objective and its key results/key initiatives and ask: "Are all these key results and key initiatives necessary?" If the answer is yes, then they pass the necessary test. If the answer is no, spend more time refining the OKRs to be more relevant and measurable.

Repeat the exercise, but this time ask: "If I accomplish all my key results and key initiatives, would I have achieved my objective?" If the answer is yes, then they pass the sufficient test. If the answer is no, you need to spend more time defining stronger key results.

10

The Most Common Questions About OKRs (and Their Answers)

Over the years, my team and I have compiled a list of the most frequently asked questions about OKRs. I'd like to share these questions—and answers—with you in case these are considerations you are wondering about, too.

What If We Don't Reach 100% of Our Goals?

In many measurement or goal frameworks, missing the target is considered a failure. OKRs, on the other hand, are about stretching past our known limits and connecting every team to the organization's purpose and business strategy. The OKR mindset encourages aspirational targets that feel slightly out of reach. A good rule of thumb is that you want to hit 70% of each aspirational OKR.

Remember that effort now pays off later. Setting strong organizational objectives provide employees with guiding principles that give them agency to operate, and as you move through the organization, outlining measurable key results gives your teams specific direction and actionable targets.

This process is about progress over perfection. The process gets easier over time, but the focus is on the behavior and the outcomes being driven as a result of the process. You're looking at the end game, not getting it right out of the gate.

We Use Agile—Why Do We Need OKRs?

Agile is an approach to project management and software development with a goal of easing the load associated with major launches by breaking work into small, consumable increments, with a continuous and iterative evaluation process baked in, so teams can adapt and respond to changes quickly.

"We are an Agile development shop. Why do we need OKRs?"

I've heard this argument countless times, especially from product and engineering organizations. But once we dig in, I've found that organizations, managers, and individuals see a natural synergy between the two philosophies, and that synergy comes from some core principles shared by both: conversation, alignment, and, of course, agility.

OKRs are a catalyst for meaningful conversations. One of the core values laid out by the Agile founders while defining their culture is "individuals and interactions over processes and tools."

To address the elephant in the room, I obviously believe in the power of tools to organize, align, and inspire a team, and, as you've seen throughout this book, I believe processes can have a massive impact on a company's culture. But none of that is successful—with any framework—if those conversations aren't present.

The second principle of the agile philosophy, alignment, is where OKRs and Agile work together so brilliantly. One of the most powerful aspects of Agile frameworks is the ability to organize cross-functional teams to work quickly together on a project. And as we know, OKRs are focused on aligning ALL projects and people to a company's biggest priorities.

The difference between the two is simple—it's about outcomes and outputs.

OKRs are outcome-focused, while Agile is output-focused.

Remember the pyramid from Chapter 1? This is a helpful tool for contextualizing how OKRs and Agile can work together so successfully.

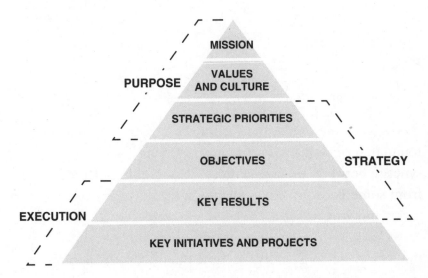

Agile is a powerful toolset for aligning, planning, scoping, and delivering projects and building features, but the strategy ("why that feature?" or "what are we trying to achieve for the business?" etc.) needs to be addressed before it becomes valuable.

This is where OKRs and Agile become so powerful. The OKR framework can organize your team to focus on the most important and ambitious priorities, and determine which work is the right work, and Agile can help your team scope and deliver on the work needed to achieve those outcomes and key initiatives, and provide measures of progress toward your OKRs.

11

Staying Focused and Tracking Progress

I've seen leaders invest heavily in the OKR creation, planning, and writing process, only to see things fall apart as their team goes back to work. How does this happen? Why does it happen? The answer is that tracking OKRs can seem arbitrary to your team without the right context and process. In this chapter, I discuss how to track progress toward OKRs to ensure that you and your team are moving forward.

The value of your key result is relative to expected progress at any given time. This can be measured in a variety of ways, from an Excel calculation to manual math, or OKR software that provides an automatic view of this "expected progress" from starting point to target value. When updates (check-ins) are made manually, the owner can add a status update focused on this expected progress and why they're behind, ahead, or on track.

The progress toward an objective should come from its key results and key initiatives, as a percentage. This will be a percentage complete, going from 0 to 100%. Remember the "necessary and sufficient" test? The key results and key initiatives should be chosen so that hitting their targets means completing the parent objective.

Scoring OKRs

At the end of a period, you'll score OKR progress to clearly contextualize period-over-period successes and failures, and enable a retrospective process that feeds planning for the next period (more on this cadence in Part III).

When scoring OKRs, you'll want to enter in any final values for key results, and the progress made on any key initiatives either as a percentage (i.e., 80% complete) or a metric (i.e., $50,000 in sales). Contextualizing OKR scores is more complex for aspirational objectives than it is for committed goals that you intended to achieve 100% on. For aspirational goals, I recommend the following scoring method:

Score	Color
≤ 0.4	Red
0.5–0.6	Orange
0.7–0.9	Green
1.0	Orange

One thing to note is that a score of 0.7 to 0.9 (70–90% complete) is considered green, or successful. For an aspirational goal (as opposed to a committed goal), it means you've gone above and beyond to succeed. Why would a perfect score of 1.0 be colored orange? The reason is that aspirational OKRs are based on stretch goals, and if you consistently reach 100% of your goals, the orange is a reminder to understand why you achieved 100% of that objective, or that you aren't setting your sights high enough.

Scoring OKRs, in general, is about context. Just like you should question why you continue to reach 100% of your "stretch" goals, you should also use your scoring exercise to ask "Why did we only reach 0.6 on these three OKRs? What do we need to do to get that up to a .08 during the next time period?"

You should score all OKRs at the end of each time period. If you complete an OKR prior to the end of a time period, you can also score it prior to the end; however, we recommend scoring all OKRs at the same time to encourage a cohesive retrospective.

Reporting and Asynchronous Communication

An important part of baking an OKR program into the culture of your business is enabling transparency and collaboration to happen outside your normal meeting cadence, when your team is able to focus.

Tamar Yehoshua, CPO of Slack, shared some thoughts on product coalition about why it's helpful to have this ability to collaborate through automation and software: "Every week, the owner of each key result gets a ping in Slack. Without leaving Slack, they can send their update directly back into [our OKR software], so that it's accurate when we share status reports in our Monday meeting."

Creating alignment, accountability, and transparency takes work, and it takes a thoughtful approach to how you share data and insight. *Insight* is a key word there. You aren't just sharing a spreadsheet of key performance indicators (KPIs).

You're creating context around the work that you're doing, and you're sharing that context on an ongoing basis.

This context should be available both asynchronously and proactively surfaced during the meeting cadence we describe in Part III.

To share information asynchronously, you'll want to create both a dashboard and a systematic approach to providing updates on a regular basis.

Asynchronous Communication and Dashboarding

Your dashboard can take many forms: a spreadsheet that you manually populate with data from multiple sources, a scrappy approach involving a few tools from your tech stack, or a centralized operating system that pulls all your data directly into your OKR score and gives you the ability to add context and external content.

Regardless of the way you manage this dashboard, you'll want to build in four specific components:

1. OKR visualization
2. A summary of your progress, plan, and problems
3. KPIs
4. A project plan

OKR Visualization

Readability is key here, so you'll want to include a concise and easy-to-consume look at how you're doing, based purely on the objectives and key results you set out to accomplish.

SCORE	COLOR
≤ 0.4	RED
0.5–0.6	ORANGE
0.7–0.9	GREEN
1.0	ORANGE

I recommend color-coding this visualization. OKR software does all of this behind the curtain, but this is also easily accomplished in Google Sheets with a little elbow grease and creativity. You want the answers to be clear, and the data to be easy to find. OKRs that are "Ahead" or "On Track" are represented with green. "Behind" is represented with yellow, and "At Risk" OKRs are represented with red.

Sharing Your Progress, Plan, and Problems

As mentioned previously, this section will incorporate your progress (what you have done), your plan (what you are going to do), and potential problems (what could negatively impact the plan).

Remembering that OKRs are focused on context and insight and not just data, your dashboard should incorporate a period-over-period look at these three areas, allowing you and your manager to review changes in status and see the full picture. I recommend doing this on a weekly basis, at least for yourself.

One mistake I've seen many people make is with the problems section. This isn't a vehicle to air your grievances. Focus on solutions. Identify the problems, identify the stakeholders you need help from, and propose a solution. The reason you took on this initiative in the first place was to be a problem-solver and create a more efficient environment. Be sure that extends to areas you feel stuck in as well. This is a valuable personal exercise.

KPIs

As I mentioned, OKRs don't replace KPIs; they complement them. Think of them as "next-level-deep" measures. When an invested party—let's say a department leader from a different part of the organization—wants to dig into a specific objective and learn more about what's making the business tick, these KPIs can prove to be valuable. They also offer supporting evidence and leading indicators when it comes to the likelihood of reaching a specific key result.

For example, there are numerous KPIs that track the development team's progress toward a specific product release. While all of them are important to deliver the product, what is important to the corporate strategy is the actual product delivery milestone. That milestone would roll up to a specific key result for the objective of a product launch. This is what matters to the success of the company, and is the event with which marketing, sales, and support need to align their deliverables.

At the same time, the sales and customer success teams want to achieve a particular objective of 98% customer satisfaction or 1% turnover. They may have as one of their KPIs to do xx QBRs and/or customer surveys. Planning and executing those may entail multiple intermediate KPIs, but the actual completion milestone would roll up to a key result that supports the corporate customer satisfaction objective.

These KPIs should be included in this dashboard to provide supporting context.

Project Plan

Your OKRs put the work you need to do in context of the results needed to move the business forward. Separating the two when reporting on OKRs is unreasonable. Just as I talk about next-level-deep KPIs, your key initiatives will be captured at the top level, as a part of your OKRs, and you can share a more detailed project plan here that adds context to your OKRs and how they'll actually be accomplished.

These plans tend to be most effective in a calendar, aligned to each key initiative. A view that allows you to see what is being worked on—and completed—by whom, and which other work it might conflict with, is important for planning, but also for tracking. "Which projects are at risk" has a direct line to "which objectives are at risk" if the planning process was effective.

Again, software can do the heavy lifting here, but Excel or a Google Sheet are also viable vehicles. Your goal is to provide enough information to give a complete picture, without over-whelming and burying what matters.

If you have included the components listed here, your dashboard may look something like this:

PROGRESS	PLAN	PROBLEMS
→ What I worked on during this time period → What I completed during this time period → What I didn't get done that I intended to	→ What I will focus on during the coming time period → Which projects and tasks I will complete during this time period → How I will make up the work that didn't get done during the last time period	→ I anticipate getting stuck on these issues These are the → stakeholders I'll need to involve to remove these problems → Here is my proposed solution to the problem

12

Wrapping Up and Reflecting on OKRs

In this chapter, we'll talk about how to create a growth mindset by reflecting, learning, and growing from your OKRs. This starts with practical applications, like scoring OKRs at the end of a period, but the most value comes from the reflection and conversation: How do you know if you were effective? Did this work make a difference? What can we learn? Scoring OKRs provides insight and accountability that adds more and more value as you grow your program.

Closing out your quarterly or annual OKRs is an important time to stop and reflect:

- What objectives did I complete successfully, and why?
- What issues did we—my team and myself—struggle with?

- Was I way too ambitious? Do I need to scale back and focus more?
- Or did I sell myself short and not set my goals high enough?
- What lessons were learned that can be applied to the next period?
- What do we want to start doing, stop doing, or continue doing in the next period?
- What OKRs can be rewritten to be more effective in the next quarter?
- What technological integrations can be added to streamline our process?
- What reports and dashboards can be created to easily track progress?
- What additional training is needed for leaders and employees?

Each time you close out your OKRs, the process becomes smoother. This is for two reasons: one is that you become more adept at staying close to your OKRs throughout the quarter or year, so there are fewer surprises and more opportunities to shift behavior mid-period to make sure your key initiatives and projects are still taking you to your OKRs—and shifting where necessary.

The second reason is that the rhythm of "close out old OKRs, set new ones" becomes a valuable, ingrained part of your routine: a pause in which you can reflect on what went as planned, what went sideways, and how you are going to take your lessons into the future on a personal and organizational level. This is part of "growing" into the growth mindset. You cease to take losses or failures personally, using them as learning mechanisms and folding them into intentional action—your next set of OKRs—as soon as possible.

The OKR program will not be successful without a commitment to making OKRs a central part of the business motion for everyone in your organization and making retrospective feedback central to your OKR process. This won't happen over-night—I take you through the phased approach I recommend in Chapter 23—but when it does, the speed at which you are able to learn from mistakes, celebrate wins, and iterate increases exponentially.

Now, feedback loops are not a new concept. Management consultant Dr. Edwards Deming created this basic model, now known as "The Deming Wheel," in the 1950s. It consists of four stages: Plan, Do, Check, and Act.

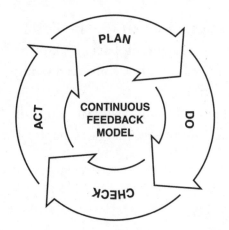

PLAN
Create an action plan for continuous feedback

DO
Execute this continuous feedback plan

CHECK
Monitor the continuous feedback plan and implement changes wherever necessary

ACT
Take necessary actions and implement the plan into the system

The continuous feedback model

What the OKR framework does with this continuous feed-back model is create a proactive and organic way for leadership, departments, teams, and individuals to participate at every stage, making goal-setting, tracking, measurement, and iteration a core component of the employee experience.

At the *Plan* stage with OKRs, you are building a plan—your key initiatives—which are always inextricably tied to your business's objectives and key results.

At the *Do* stage with OKRs, you are in execution mode, but consistently referring back to your OKRs. In practice, this might look like including a mini OKR review in each team meeting and/or 1:1, automating your check-ins using your OKR software, or regular leadership updates at Town Halls using OKRs as a focal point. You're giving feedback and making changes as you go along, as opposed to "set it and forget it," which we know doesn't work.

At the *Check* stage with OKRs, you are checking in with formalized milestones in the time period you are using, whether it's a quarter or a year. This is giving you a "forced" (but welcome!) entrypoint into your progress, and a chance to pivot as necessary.

Finally, you reach the *Act* stage, in which you are finalizing your results from the time period, stepping back, looking at them, and making actionable choices for how you are moving forward based on the new information.

Using OKRs as part of your continuous feedback loop, all the elements in the pyramid I shared at the beginning of Chapter 1 are put under the microscope.

For instance, did my marketing campaign fail to hit its key results because my targets were too lofty, or because the campaign itself wasn't aligned to our company's mission and strategic priorities, and thus failed to resonate with our audience?

Another question that I might ask is, what went wrong in setting these targets for key results? Was there a problem with the data I was using? When these key results were finalized with my team and/or leadership, was there an understanding that they would be stretch goals, or was there agreement that they should absolutely be achievable?

Unlike the old way of doing things, where strategy cascades down and ultimately both leadership and most employees lose line of sight, a modern-day OKR process involves a holistic view of the business that goes both top-to-bottom and bottom-up. OKRs in the twenty-first century encourage and, in my mind, *require* active involvement from everyone in the organization, from planning, doing, checking, and acting in one cycle to planning the next.

Rules for Reflection

There are three primary rules to ensure that feedback loops are established for teams and departments:

1. **Establish feedback rhythms**
   This process won't happen on its own. Feedback and retrospectives should be regular and continuous, each period. Be sure that there is a documented application of feedback. A *Forbes* study found that 75% of employees crave honest feedback,[1] but fewer than one-third actually receive it. Feedback is important for each individual's career development,

---

[1]Victor Lipman, "65% of Employees Want More Feedback (So Why Don't They Get It?)," *Forbes*, August 8, 2016, https://www.forbes.com/sites/victorlipman/2016/08/08/65-of-employees-want-more-feedback-so-why-dont-they-get-it/?sh=30388758914a.

but also for the teams and programs you're running, and the progress you're making toward your objectives.

2. **Remove bias**

    Feedback loops should be based in data. Using this process to confirm beliefs or bias is an unproductive use of time. On the contrary—the goal should be to challenge the beliefs and biases you have. Without that challenge, you'll continue to operate under these assumptions, so the feedback loop wouldn't be necessary.

3. **Record feedback**

    As a general rule, document your progress and feedback. This is a critical component of transparency, and will make future reviews more effective.

13

Company OKRs

With the framework for how to build and structure your OKRs, you can begin drafting your own and cascading them throughout your department. You're almost ready to move into Part III of this book, which is focused on creating the right rhythms and processes to enable OKRs to drive your business forward.

But before we do that, I thought it would be helpful to share examples my team has seen. In this section, you'll find dozens of OKRs to inspire your own writing process. Let's start with company OKRs, and move into department-specific considerations, benefits, challenges, and examples.

What Are Good Company OKRs?

As you set up your company OKRs, it's great to build them around initiatives such as:

- Hiring and employee growth initiatives
- Marketing lead and pipeline contribution
- Marketing-led initiatives such as rebranding, events, or design
- Sales revenue targets and market expansion
- Product-led initiatives such as new versions, updates, or features
- Service initiatives such as support request metrics, handling time, or improved efficiency

Annual Company-Level OKR Examples

Objective: Expand into the Latin American market.
   Key Results:

- Capture 15% of LATAM market share from our competitors.
- Hire and train four bilingual sales executives by February 10th.
- Launch Spanish-language MVP version of product with top five requested features.

   Key Initiative:

- Campaign targeting key personas in Latin American countries.

Objective: Achieve record revenue while maintaining profitability.

Key Results:

- Increase sales of new enterprise-level accounts from $31 million to $50 million.
- Expand add-on service revenue from existing customers from $12 million to $22 million.
- Maintain 10–11% profit margins.

Key Initiatives:

- Audit software spend.
- Public launch of new product line.

Objective: Host a live virtual event for 1,000 customers in September to drive expansion opportunities.

Key Results:

- Reach 1,000 registrants for the event by the end of Q2.
- Set 100 live demo meetings.
- $25 million in expansion revenue attributed to the event by EOY.

Key Initiatives:

- Launch new product in keynote session.
- Host private dinner with key customers.

Quarterly Company-Level OKR Examples

Objective: Become a "must have" product.
Key Results:

- Grow from 2,000 to 5,000 users.
- Attain 4,500 engaged users.
- Achieve 90% MAU in user base.

Key Initiative:

- Develop customer council to inform new product decisions.

Objective: Reach $100 million in ARR.
Key Results:

- Drive $25 million in new bookings.
- Drive $25 million in expansion bookings.
- Retain 95% of customers Q/Q.

Key Initiatives:

- Launch ABM campaign in key vertical.
- In-product upsell initiative.

Objective: Grow company twofold.
Key Results:

- Expand company from 250 to 500 employees.
- Retain 100% of employees Q/Q.

Key Initiative:

- Host all-company event.

14

OKRs for Each Department

Each department in your organization plays a specific role. By aligning the work each department does and collaborating cross-functionally, these departments can help move the needle on the business's most important goals. But more often than not, they end up working in silos, which leads to chaos and hinders the success of the organization.

Without alignment and clarity, teams are unable to productively contribute to the business's topline goals, and wind up creating their own definitions of success, which can be wildly different from one another. We've established the role that OKRs play in solving this process. OKRs bring alignment across the organization, and, when applied with the loose approach discussed throughout this book, the differences between these departments becomes less of a challenge to overcome and more of a strength to harness.

In this chapter, you'll learn some of these department-specific nuances, and the benefits OKRs bring to their specific functions, but I'll also detail some of the challenges these departments and leaders within them can expect to face as they participate in their organization's OKR practice.

If you're a departmental leader, my hope for you is that by the end of this section, you'll be better equipped to address the specific needs of your role and your team as you embark on the next phase of your OKR journey.

The Strategy and Operations Team

Often, a strategy and operations team is responsible for a company's OKR practice by default. These teams and their leaders own the rhythm of the business, the processes and systems, and the strategic direction of the company. OKRs help strategy and operations leaders bring the rest of the company into that process, and make sure information and work doesn't break down between departments and tools.

OKR Benefits for the Strategy and Operations Team

For strategy and operations teams, the goal of an OKR program is going to be similar to that of the business, given that is their department's charge. But there are practical advantages that strategy and ops leaders find from the system.

1. **Align Cross-Departmentally for Timely Solutions:** The business operations team is often tasked with bringing

teams together to create and execute a plan that addresses a core business need. OKRs create the structure to align work across multiple functions, and provide visibility and direction to everyone involved, by adding time-bound goals, milestones, and metrics to otherwise disparate plans.

2. **Standardize Process:** One of the largest complaints you'll hear from a chief operating officer or other business operations leader is that processes aren't standardized. The product team uses agile sprints and DevOps or Jira. Sales uses quarterly quotas and Microsoft Dynamics or Salesforce. Marketing plans biannually and uses too many software solutions to remember. Bringing all of this together can be daunting. OKRs don't try to create one system for every piece of work and every bit of information. What they do is organize work around the most important outcomes your business needs to drive, and highlight the most important information you need to move the business forward.

Challenges and How to Address Them

Because the strategy and ops team is focused on cross-departmental work, there are unique challenges for them that don't exist for other departments. In this section, I outline the most common of those challenges and how to address them.

Challenge: Aligning teams to collaborate cross-functionally and drive the outcomes that matter to the business is a daunting undertaking. Bringing different processes, understandings, and ways of working together into one approach isn't always feasible, but creating a shared understanding can be.

Solution: Since the operations team glues all departments together, they are often found running from pillar to post to get work done. Having OKRs helps them get clarity on what needs to be done and helps them pass this clarity on to the different departments, aligning them to the broader goals and boosting cross-functional collaboration.

Challenge: Having to manually create and distribute OKR materials and facilitate the entire OKR process with the various departments is both tedious and time-consuming, creating bottlenecks and extra work for your team.

Solution: OKR software helps with every aspect of this challenge, from creation of OKRs, distribution, updates, and reminders. If extra work is standing in the way of transparency and collaboration, I highly recommend the investment.

Challenge: Operations teams frequently build OKR performance reports and dashboards for other teams, who turn to them for reporting and insights on new key processes or initiatives. This becomes outdated quickly and often requires rework.

Solution: Automate the process. An investor I've worked with used to say, "If you have to do it more than once, build a system to do it for you." OKR software will connect to your data, remind teams to check in, and automate the entire process when possible.

How to Connect OKRs to Operations Team Rhythms and Tools

For more on how strategy and operations professionals can successfully become the glue that holds the company together, I turned to a long-time operations leader to learn from his experience.

BizOps: The Lynchpin Team

Atul Sahai, Strategy and Operations Leader

Business operations teams are at the core of a well-run business. The team brings other functions and departments together and asks the question, does what you're doing make sense for the business? In this blog, I'll dive into the challenges BizOps teams face and how they can succeed with goal setting through OKRs.

Business Operations Challenges

I believe the two biggest challenges BizOps teams face are setting the right context and creating the right amount of structure for the company.

As companies grow, and grow fast, the challenge becomes how do you keep this connective tissue going? How do you make sure that everyone's team goals are aligned? That's where OKRs come in. It's not about command and control. With OKRs, you set the context, and people, in a very ideal world, grab the context and run fast.

The context setting is key for success. Many times, everyone in the company might be saying the same thing, but some teams or individuals may be interpreting the message a little bit differently. Setting the right context and making sure everybody grasps it is one of the challenges and opportunities for a business—you can put it both ways.

Setting Your OKR Structure

When it comes to structure, especially in a fast-growth company, we are trying to bring in some structure amid the chaos.

(continued)

However, how much organization is another question. If your business is in a very steady state and there is a very set rhythm, structure makes sense. But in our case, we are growing our employee count 25% to 30% every quarter. You have to bring employees in with some organization, but there should be a tension between how much structure you impose versus some beauty in the chaos as well. If you make your business too structured, it will inhibit growth and creativity.

Scaling without Nailing It

If you don't nail the concept or rhythm of your operating principles, and you try to scale too fast, it's not going to work. For example, a very top-down mandated approach to OKRs typically fails.

In my past experience, I've had situations where I've done OKRs and the approach has been to immediately roll the framework out to every single employee. Thankfully we didn't do that. You need to start with the core, get it solid, and then grow around it.

Not Evolving as the Business Is Evolving

If we believe that how we operate with 20 employees and $1 million in revenue is the same as how we will operate at $100 million, then that is a recipe for disaster.

Business operations teams have to keep changing and evolving. In my past life, within two or three years at the same company, we used three different goal methodologies for running business operations. You just outgrow some and at some point you realize it isn't clicking. Especially early on, if you're trying to impose a process that is very bureaucratic, then you have to focus more of your time on doing the thing rather than managing the process. That's not good, but as you evolve, you have to start laying on more structure.

Important Management Styles for BizOps Leaders

One of the most important qualities a BizOps leader needs to have is the ability to collaborate. I don't mean making decisions by consensus, although sometimes you have to do that. I mean collaboration—you're really that connective tissue across a lot of functions. OKR can be a monumentally helpful resource for this collaboration, because they foster discussion. Enable these discussions whenever possible.

Leaders who have the "my way or the highway" approach are not going to be successful. People are not going to gravitate toward whatever you want them to do or whatever process you want.

It's important to have the flexibility and growth mindset for testing and iterating. Be willing to fail and learn and iterate. BizOps leaders should obviously be analytical, have a structured thought process, and be methodical, but intangibles like flexibility and being collaborative are key.

Why BizOps Teams Should Use OKRs for Goal Setting

BizOps has the unique vantage point where they can see the lay of the land and the entire business to understand where people resources and investments are going, and what the outputs are.

BizOps is especially suited to work with OKRs because there is a structured process, whether it is top down or bottom up. That's where OKRs really fit in. Trying to bring some structure to the chaos.

(continued)

BizOps is meant to bring a lot of collaboration, alignment, and transparency to organizations, which is an evolu-
tion that's happened in the past 10–20 years. Earlier you would
have these silos. Product would make the product, marketing
would figure out to market the product . . . especially in SaaS,
the lines between product marketing and sales are blurred. So
in that sense you need alignment and transparency, and that's
where I think OKRs help to bring that in across departments.

OKRs also help with the rhythm of the business. How
are we doing check-ins and are we progressing toward our
goals and learning from them?

How to Get Started Rolling Out OKRs for the First Time

When you're first getting started with OKRs, don't roll them
out to everyone before you decide why you are doing it.

In my past experience rolling out OKRs to a team,
team members were quick to connect OKRs to performance reviews, which is not what we want. We don't want
to be a "big brother." The objective is different.

Everybody wants to go from 0 to 60 very quickly, but
make sure the people side has been sorted out and everyone
understands why you're doing OKRs. Make sure to explain
the problem the team is trying to solve and what problem is
going to be solved with the OKR.

The nice thing that comes out of OKRs is everybody
starts to see how to think about the business in a structured way and see who is doing what and highlighting
those benefits.

If you have never done OKRs, or want to test it out,
don't go very big right away. Start with a smaller pilot

group, department, or leadership team and make sure it works before going bigger.

Lastly, make sure to build a rhythm around the process. It's not something you set and forget. You need to have a cadence and just don't make it an exercise for people to check in. Clearly show how it's helping the business.

The goal of OKRs is to not have met the goal. The goal is to figure out how we can improve the business, invest more or less, rather than getting fixated on the mechanics.

It can take a while to get there, but get into the mindset that the goal is not to do OKRs better, the goal is to execute the business better.

Ensuring a BizOps OKR Program Doesn't Fail

Sometimes we hear customers say that they don't have key results, they just have projects that roll up to the objectives. This is completely fine, just make sure to figure out where individuals will work and make it flexible.

An OKR program can fail if individuals feel like it's just more work to do. That's where having the right tool comes in. Good OKR software has robust integrations so people aren't just punching in numbers from one system to another. If people feel like it's busy work, it will fail.

Lastly, OKRs are not going to solve everything for the business, and you can't go into it with that mentality.

Figure out exactly what you're trying to solve for and bring OKRs in. Putting in a system won't solve the problem. The culture and the tool you bring in, and the processes they have, all have to work together.

Sometimes the software drives the culture, sometimes the culture will determine the software. Just make sure all of those things are in harmony.

Sample OKRs for the Operations Team

Next, I share some sample OKRs for strategy and operations teams. Keep in mind that these are examples meant to inspire creative thinking on your team, not to serve as OKRs for you to cut and paste. Your business has specific needs that only you and your team are aware of.

Chief Operating Officer OKR Examples

Chief operating officer OKRs are responsible for your overall business strategy and comprehensive goals. It's important that COOs set the stage by properly creating goals and OKRs that their team can follow.

What Are Good COO OKRs?   As you set up your COO OKRs it's great to build them around initiatives such as:

- Hiring initiatives geared toward growth
- Expansion of overall business strategy into new territories and geographical areas
- Total revenue growth and revenue growth in specific territories
- Product-related goals such as awards
- New user acquisition for products

COO OKR Examples for Business Expansion

- **Objective:** Expand the business nationally to generate more revenue.
- **Key Results**
  - Hire 25 new employees across sales, marketing, and customer success.

- Launch seven geographical marketing campaigns targeting our ICPs.
- Generate $10 million in sales outside Southeast territory.
- Onboard 200 new mid-market customers in the West and Central region.
- **Key Initiative:**
  - Launch employer brand campaign.
- **Objective:** Expand the business globally to generate more revenue in key territories.
- **Key Results**
  - Hire 10 new SDRs to penetrate UK and EMEA markets.
  - Generate $6.7 million in sales pipeline during the quarter.
  - Onboard 25 new customers in UK and EMEA markets.
- **Key Initiatives:**
  - Launch geotargeted marketing campaigns targeting our ICPs.
  - Conduct full analysis of new target geos.

COO OKR Example for Product Expansion

- **Objective:** Increase product footprint.
- **Key Results**
  - Identify and secure 150+ channel resellers.
  - Grow our freemium user base from 0 to 1 million active users.
  - Gain 2 million active new paid users.
  - Increase average time in product from 5 minutes to 10 minutes.
- **Key Initiative:**
  - Launch self-serve onboarding.

COO OKR Example for Diversity and Hiring

- **Objective:** Increase the diversity of our company.
- **Key Results**
  - Increase gender diversity of leadership positions to 40%.
  - Remove gender bias from 100% of job descriptions.
  - Ensure 100% of recruiting loops include representation from multiple races.
- **Key Initiative:**
  - Host job fairs in culturally diverse settings.

Chief of Staff Goals and Objectives Examples

The chief of staff is a cross-functional role that is responsible for communicating and strategizing with the CEO. The chief of staff must be nimble and help align strategy and goals across all departments.

What Are Good Chief of Staff Goals and OKRs?   As you set up your chief of staff OKRs, build them around initiatives such as:

- Company alignment
- Hiring and growth initiatives
- Budget planning
- Establishing company-wide goals and KPIs

Chief of Staff OKR Examples Related to Alignment

- **Objective:** Implement regular usage of OKRs by end of quarter to increase alignment.
- **Key Results**
  - Introduce OKRs and train 100% of employees on benefits, rhythm, expectations, and process.

- Ensure that 100% of departments create and finalize OKRs.
- Ensure that 100% of employees are performing weekly check-ins.
- Score 100% of OKRs by EOQ.
- **Key Initiatives:**
- Redefine core company rhythms.
- Establish DEI council.

Chief of Staff OKR Examples Related to Productivity

- **Objective:** Maximize productivity through more efficient business practices.
- **Key Results**
- Finish all scheduled meetings 15 minutes early.
- Automate five manual business practices by end of quarter.
- Increase goal achievement score from 68% to 90%.
- **Key Initiative:**
- Establish new meeting cadence across the company.

OKRs for Operations Leadership

- **Objective:** Decrease cash burn QoQ in order to keep the company financially stable.
- **Key Results**
- Consolidate internal work tools to decrease monthly spend from $12,000 to $8,000.
- Increase employees working full time from home from 20% to 50% of workforce.
- Lower monthy cash burn from $1.5 million per month to $1.2 million per month.

- **Key Initiatives:**
  - Audit internal SaaS subscriptions.
  - Meet with each department head to assess hiring plan necessity.
- **Objective:** Accelerate business growth through strategy and insights.
- **Key Results**
  - Achieve 500 active users on our V1 business data platform.
  - Consolidate sources to visualize and consume key business insights from five sources to two sources.
  - Reduce time to create quarterly board of advisors presentation from five days to two days.
- **Key Initiative:**
  - Department needs assessment process.
- **Objective:** Scale our company operations efficiently and effectively in order to better serve our customers and employees.
- **Key Results**
  - Double supply chain capacity while maintaining operational excellence.
  - Achieve 16% profit margin through production efficiencies.
  - Increase our operations department headcount by 10%.
- **Key Initiative:**
  - Implement new production process that eliminates unnecessary steps.

The Product Team

Product teams and product leaders are responsible for building the best customer experience by listening to customer feedback and continuously innovating and improving upon every feature they—along with engineering or manufacturing groups—build. The OKR framework is critical for product teams to plan and articulate the product's direction in such a way that it stays focused on the larger goals of the business, and provides a clear line of sight into how that connection is made.

OKR Benefits for the Product Team

Since OKRs were born and raised in technology companies like Intel and Google, it won't surprise you that the benefits they bring to a product division are numerous. OKRs are—by nature—designed to create a common language across a company, and that is a necessary function in any fast-moving and ever-changing industry in which businesses are expected to develop new products and iterate on current ones. In this section, you'll find several of these benefits that we've seen after working with thousands of companies, but, as you build your own program, you'll undoubtedly uncover more.

1. Focus Product Direction

With OKRs, product teams plan based on the outcomes they need the product to achieve, with the business's most important goals at the center of that planning. Without a framework for organizing, product roadmaps can become a collection of disparate plans to address unfocused needs, whether those needs are driven by customer requests, reactive responses to sentiment and usage, or gut feelings and ideas. When applied thoughtfully, the OKR framework creates a connective thread that runs through the entire roadmap and a need for research and validation that may otherwise be overlooked.

2. **Clear Communication of Progress**

With OKRs, product leaders are able to clearly articulate the impact being made at any given point in time. By establishing the right measures for products that are in development, milestones, and aligning project plans, the work being done is clearly aligned to purpose, simplified with a high-level summary, and easy to break down into "next level" detail.

3. **Alignment to Company Goals**

Aligning product to a revenue or customer retention goal can feel daunting. There are so many other factors that go into company goals at that elevation. That's the magic that OKRs bring. Those revenue and customer targets, especially when designed to stretch your team, take a concerted effort, and that effort is impossible without the product at the center of it.

4. **Proactively Identify Risks and Blockers**

If you've ever planned a product roadmap, you've likely also had to adjust that roadmap due to unforeseen issues, delays, and urgent requests from customers or your sales team. These risks will continue to show up. The OKR process, when used as a part of your regular business rhythms with frequent check-ins, will help you stay ahead of those risks and blockers. If the sales team is behind on their new revenue objective, you may need to get creative to help close a deal. Conversely, if a bug is delaying a product release, you'll recognize this quickly, and be able to assess with your peers how this will impact the OKRs for other areas of the business.

5. **Shed Light on Dependencies and Promote Cross-Functional Collaboration**

Product teams sit at the center of the organization and work closely with every department. OKRs and the process of creating them as a company will give you the insight you need to discover and address cross-functional dependencies. What sales goals are contingent on product delivery? Which marketing or customer success plans should be changed based on your roadmap? These questions are answered through the iterative approach of writing OKRs as a company.

Challenges and How to Address Them

Like anything, there are challenges that will arise from change. When implementing an OKR practice, you can expect challenges that are specific to product departments.

Challenge: Many product teams face an inability to keep project status current in a way that is meaningful beyond their team. This impacts visibility into progress toward the impact you're working to make, both for the stakeholders who need that visibility to be successful in their own functions, and for your own team.

Solution: As a part of your regular rhythms, I've found product teams are more successful when leaders promote regular check-ins and use OKRs as a key part of team meetings. This keeps the focus on the outcome, not each individual task or card within a sprint. Track your OKR and workflow progress using connected systems so that progress toward product goals and progress made in everyday work connect to one another seamlessly, and ideally, automatically.

Challenge: Creating measurable key results when the team is used to sprints and delivery timelines can be tricky. In a binary approach, OKRs are more difficult to leverage. You're not able to track and evaluate progress when the core metric is either "incomplete" or "complete."

Solution: Turn the core initiatives your product team is working on into project plans that roll up to an OKR, so you can measure progress toward key results via progress made on your workback schedule. The key milestones in that workback schedule are how you'll track whether you're on track to meet your objective.

How to Connect OKRs to Product Team Rhythms and Tools

I discussed in Chapter 10 how OKRs and Agile methodologies work together. This is an important construct for many product teams who rely on Agile principles for development cycles. To bridge that gap, I asked a product leader I've worked with for years to share his experience.

Connecting "What" to "Why"

Balaji Seetharaman, Product Management Leader

We often get asked, "Our engineering team feels like OKRs are too redundant with their Agile structure using Azure DevOps or Jira as a tool; what do we do?"

While tools like this provide a way to plan and manage tasks, OKRs connect "why" the work is being done and ensure that the work is connected to the company's most important goals.

For teams I've led, I believe there have been three stages to the OKR journey.

Stage 1: We use DevOps predominantly as a planning tool for sprints and lists of tasks. What's not connected here is the "why" behind the work we are doing and what the work is connected to. So I asked myself, how do I make the work motivating for my teams? The answer is, a lot of it comes from connecting the day-to-day tasks to the bigger vision and goals. So we created goals like "do X with high quality" or "do X with high predictability" and focused on how we were innovating while still doing the work. It worked all right, but our work as the product department was still siloed from the rest of the company.

Stage 2: We established our key initiatives at the team level that everyone was contributing to with metrics related to the work. So we had high-level OKRs that connected with projects at the team level, but nothing in between. It brought alignment to our team, but still wasn't connecting work and goals at every level.

Stage 3: Stage 3 is where we are at now, and have found the most value for OKRs. We've established our team OKRs, which are typically lag metrics and something you would only know at the end of the cycle whether or not it was accomplished. But this time we also defined the lead metrics along the way to ensure we are regularly measuring whether the work we are doing is helping us get closer to accomplishing our goals. That's why every week, our product teams update the status of projects and OKRs and review what they accomplished in the previous week, what is planned for the following week, and what we are doing to get closer to the input metrics even though we haven't achieved the lag metric.

(*continued*)

This also provides an opportunity for every team member to connect their work to not only their team's mission but the company's overall mission. We ask ourselves, are we doing the right set of tasks every agile sprint? If you're documenting only in DevOps or Jira, you won't get that context.

By connecting goals to our daily work, we've improved our focus in terms of how we are building features out, how we are collaborating, and how we keep focused on results while executing our projects. We've gotten into this rhythm of reviewing OKRs every week and connecting the work to the goals on a regular basis, and it's truly changed the way we operate.

Sample OKR for the Product Team

OKR Examples for Product Leadership

- **Objective:** Deliver a "must have" product in order to delight customers and grow our user base.
- **Key Results**
  - Increase our NPS score from 40 to 50.
  - Increase daily active users (DAUs) from 1,200 to 1,500.
  - Drive 1,000 downloads.
- **Key Initiative:**
  - Launch mobile app to customer base and market.
- **Objective:** Launch 2.0 version of product in order to fix bugs, refine UI, and drive user engagement.
- **Key Results**
  - Reduce number of support tickets from 120/month to 30/month.
  - Reduce number of steps in check out process from 9 to 6.

- Increase user time spent on site from 2:37 per session to 3:45 per session.
- **Key Initiative:**
- Publish in-app guide feature.

OKR Examples for Product Managers

- **Objective:** Increase NPS score in order to retain our best customers and attract new ones.
- **Key Results**
  - Increase our NPS from 84 to 91.
  - Achieve a 98% customer renewal rate.
  - Attract 1,000 new customer leads through product features.
- **Key Initiative:**
  - Follow up with every NPS survey below 84 to understand opportunities for growth.

The Human Resources Team

The HR leader is an important participant in the implementation and rollout of an OKR program, and they have a unique lens into what makes a practice like this successful. While not directly responsible for revenue or product development, the HR team has a vested interest in the success of every employee, every team, and the business as a whole.

OKR Benefits for the HR Team

While the HR team is generally responsible for performance management programs and employee engagement, often, an OKR program is rolled out at the department or leadership level.

This doesn't mean HR should be left out of the loop. They are an important stakeholder and a critical lynchpin for gaining buy-in and developing the right process and balance. Here are some frequent benefits of OKRs that I've seen for HR departments:

1. **Engagement:** As you've read to this point, OKRs create a culture of engaged employees through participation. This is a critical metric for many HR teams. When employees are engaged and involved in conversations that aren't directly about their specific role, they feel more connected to the business and their colleagues, which increases retention and productivity.

2. **Change Management:** Businesses go through frequent periods of change. Market shifts, organizational alignment changes, management turnover, and new product development are just a few factors that can impact how business is done and how employees are forced to rethink their contribution. OKRs add clarity, which becomes a critical tool during any period of change.

3. **Focus:** While HR teams aren't responsible for the work every employee is doing and where they spend their energy, they often find themselves acting as a counselor when employees are frustrated with their job. OKRs focus every employee on the most important work they can be doing and give the HR team a lens into what that work is so that they can offer clearer guidance and support.

4. **Onboarding:** OKRs ease onboarding by offering a structure through which a new employee can view the business's focus and ambition, which they can then explore deeper and see how each department and team contribute to that focus. This structure paints a clear picture, and gives context to conversations they'll have with other colleagues as a part of their onboarding.

5. **Career Growth:** OKRs are not meant to be tied to compensation, which can feel like a tricky balance for many HR leaders, but as I mentioned before, OKRs can be an input to performance conversations, because they focus on outcomes and impact, and add context to the impact that person has made beyond the KPIs that their compensation is tied to. Performance should go beyond the minimum bar that employee is trying to cross that quarter, and focus on their growth and satisfaction with their work.

Challenges and How to Address Them

Like with anything, there are challenges that will arise from change. When implementing an OKR practice, you can expect challenges that are specific to human resources departments.

Challenge: Engaging frontline workers, and those who work in regionally specific roles, can be difficult, as can communicating the company objectives, how their work contributes to them, and how they're progressing, but that doesn't make it any less important to create that connection.

Solution: Include OKRs in the conversations during field visits to help employees gain clarity on what the company's goals are and how their daily work moves the needle on those goals. In the era of smartphones, even employees who aren't working at a desk every day can stay connected with the right enablement. Encourage employees to use the mobile version of your OKR tool so that they can stay connected and understand how their work ties to the overarching goals. This will boost accountability and excitement about their contribution, and also help them stay connected to their colleagues, which adds visibility into the work that they're doing as well.

Challenge: Onboarding has undergone a series of major changes in the hybrid world, where a new employee can't be physically escorted around an office to meet colleagues, highlight resources, and gain context into what will be expected of them.

Solution: Provide new employees access to past and current OKRs, and ask them to share a summary of what they learn by digging in. This will help employees understand company goals and how you aim to achieve them. Another tactic I've seen work well is to include your annual, half-yearly, and quarterly OKRs in your company playbook to provide new folks the direction that they need.

Challenge: Company culture is more than an HR program, but it's one that HR leaders generally champion. Developing a great culture for the organization is harder now than ever before. Hybrid and remote work have nullified many in-office traditions and rituals, and employees feel disconnected from everyone, including their direct manager, in many cases.

Solution: By establishing OKRs that keep employee engagement and career development at their core, you won't necessarily regain the organic aspects of culture we once saw, but an intentional culture will have a stronger impact on employee experience. I also recommend that you add continuous performance management into your company rhythms and rituals. Annual reviews are great for focusing important conversations, but much of what happens in those conversations should happen throughout the year, too.

Challenge: Striking the right balance between OKRs and performance management can be confusing to employees and can create a perception issue around your OKR program if not done with the correct context and approach.

Solution: Curb the urge to tie OKRs to compensation and instead use OKRs to steer open conversations that help employees reflect and continuously improve their performance. Not only will they gain a morale boost through recognition of their efforts rather than results, but this will foster a growth mindset that benefits both employee and the business as a whole.

How to Connect to Department-Specific Rhythms

In today's climate, burnout is top of mind for many HR teams. This is a major issue that impacts productivity, retention, and the ability to forecast. OKRs, as a part of a thoughtful mindset about the employee experience, can help combat this. I asked an HR leader I've worked with to share some thoughts about this very topic with several experts.

Reducing Burnout with Clarity

Rebecca Clements, Human Resources Leader

Employee burnout doesn't just happen overnight. It's a culmination of stress—physical or emotional—over time that results in employees feeling dispassionate, disengaged, cynical, and unproductive (just to name a few). Unfortunately, the past two years have presented employees with plenty of triggers that, by now, have resulted in historically high levels of burnout. According to Asana, 71% of workers experienced burnout in 2021, and 42% rate their stress level as "high" or "very high."[1]

And yet, a whopping 85% of employees don't think their company is doing enough to address the issue.

I recently gathered people leaders together to discuss ways their organizations have been tackling this phenomenon:

(*continued*)

[1] Asana, "Anatomy of Work Report, 2021," https://resources.asana.com/rs/784-XZD-582/images/PDF-FY21-Global-EN-Anatomy%20of%20Work%20Report.pdf.

- Derek Schlicker—Chief Financial Officer at Quantivate
- Melissa Isaza—Director of People & Culture at Unbounce
- Megan Pawlak—Director of People & Culture at Apeel Sciences
- Stacey Carroll—Director of Human Resources at TKK

1. Have leaders set an example to reduce employee burnout?

There are only so many human resource partners to go around in a day. Magnify your impact by doubling down on time spent with leaders.

"Empower your managers and people leaders to have authentic conversations with employees and allow people to be human," says Megan, Director of People & Culture at Apeel Sciences.

Remind them to start meetings with a simple "How are you?" instead of diving straight into business. Beyond that, encourage leaders to model the behavior you want to see take hold across the organization.

Want people to take PTO? Then get your leaders to unplug from time to time. Want people speaking honestly about their mental health? Then give leaders the tools and guidance to start these conversations with their teams.

2. Create a common language around feelings.

Don't ignore the reality that emotions can and will contribute to company culture, employee decision making, and productivity. Instead, find a way to hold space for emotion and feelings within the organization. Doing this, Stacey Carroll, Director of Human Resources at TKK, says, "eliminate[s] the shame . . . that comes with feeling like 'I'm the only one [experiencing burnout], everyone else already has this figured out.'"

Melissa Isaza, Director of People & Culture at Unbounce, recommends that companies "create a common language and name feelings that people can feel connected to so they don't feel alone."

Her company, Unbounce, has adopted a common language, where employees share whether they're feeling above or below "the line"—with feelings of being below often aligning with feelings of burnout. This practice allows employees to be honest about how they're showing up to work in that moment, without having to divulge or specify potentially private feelings.

Finally, it can be incredibly powerful to simply remind employees that burnout isn't failure. It's a natural consequence of prolonged, demanding activity that would cause even the most amazing, rock star employee to feel stressed and—ultimately—burned out.

3. Set employee and goal expectations.

According to the Mayo Clinic, one of the major reasons for employee burnout stems from unclear job expectations. It makes sense—if you don't understand how your work is connected to organization goals, or if you're not even clear about what's expected of you, then it follows that you'd feel disillusioned, unsatisfied, and lack the energy to be productive (all classic signs of burnout).

(continued)

In 2021, 29% of employees surveyed for Asana's Anatomy of Work report said a lack of clarity on tasks and roles was a top factor fueling their burnout. The solution? 34% said the main thing that will motivate them to do their best work is knowing how their work contributes to the company's overall mission.

That is the power of objectives and key results (OKRs). When organization goals are clearly laid out and cascade down to departments and teams, employees will know exactly how and what they're expected to contribute, and by when. This promotes ownership of their piece of the business and gives employees a reason to work hard because they can see exactly how their work connects to the company's mission.

4. Adjust your PTO policy to reduce burnout.

Encourage your employees to take a well-deserved break. Melissa suggests renaming paid time off (PTO) to reduce the stigma around taking a mental health day. Instead of differentiating "sick" and "mental health" days, combine the two into simply "wellness" days, so employees are empowered to utilize their time off to take care of their physical and mental well-being. To ensure they can actually reap the benefits of this time off and truly unplug, Derek Schlicker, Chief Financial Officer at Quantivate, emphasizes the need to put support in place to get the work done on their behalf.

Can't totally revamp your PTO policy? Start small! I suggest embracing holidays that span your distributed workforce. In my current company, we've adopted two Labor Days, India's and the United States', and these are recognized as holidays across both teams.

Pro tip: If you have unlimited PTO, set a minimum expectation so employees don't have to guess and stress about what's a "normal" amount of time to take off. Just tell them!

5. Prioritize (but actually).

From that same Asana survey, 46% of employees cited being overworked as a key factor fueling their burnout. Managers should be actively working to rid your organization of overwhelming workloads that lead to employee burnout. How?

Stacey encourages her leaders to start meetings with a brainstorm of what they can get rid of, because "you're only able to address priorities if you can also figure out what to stop doing."

Melissa's team takes Nora Roberts's approach to juggling it all. In a Q&A on how she balances writing and kids, the author shared a key nugget of wisdom: "The key to juggling is to know that some of the balls you have in the air are made of plastic and some are made of glass."

Since inevitably some will drop, make sure your team knows which balls will bounce and which ones will shatter so they can prioritize accordingly.

6. Connect before content.

Stacey pointed to a quote from an SHRM [Society for Human Resource Management] interview with Scott Galloway, where he maintains that "we are a long way from creating the technical equivalent of an in-person interaction, and likely will never capture the serendipity of the casual workplace interaction."[2]

(*continued*)

---

[2]David Ward, "Post-Coronavirus: A Q&A with Scott Galloway," SHRM, March 4, 2021, https://www.shrm.org/hr-today/news/hr-magazine/spring2021/pages/post-corona-scott-galloway-interview.aspx.

While that may be true, we can still try to recreate the serendipity of "water cooler" talk.

Start every meeting with connection, not content—ask your colleagues how they're doing. Is there someone you used to bump into in the hall or grab coffee with that you haven't connected with for a while? Shoot them a message.

Megan suggests making an effort to get outside your immediate team and connect with cross-functional partners you haven't seen in a while. These simple acts of connection can go a long way in reversing employee burnout.

7. Block out time.

Avoid Zoom fatigue by eliminating unnecessary meetings and giving your team time back for focused work. Many organizations today are blocking out meeting-free time—company-wide—on the calendar.

Apeel is so committed to this idea that they set a company-wide objective to reduce the time everyone's spending in meetings. Employees can use their "productivity pods" to accomplish whatever needs to be done. Some days that's work, others it's grocery shopping. We do this at our company, too, freeing up a few afternoons each week for folks to turn off their cameras, regain their sanity, and focus on the tasks that will help them achieve key results.

8. Record meetings.

Record your meetings so employees can listen in after the fact. This can be a saving grace for parents who have to jump offline mid-afternoon to pick up kids from school or whose toddler decided to have a meltdown two minutes before an important call. This simple tactic comes in handy for any employee who finds themselves in a situation where life interrupts their Zoom calls.

9. Reduce burnout by embracing flexibility and creativity.

One of the most effective ways to reduce employee burnout is to embrace scheduling flexibility. Stacey reminds us of the basics: employees are individuals, and what works for one won't work for the next.

In research from the *Harvard Business Review*, 32% of employees surveyed say they never want to return to working in the office, while another 21% say they never want to spend another day working from home.[3]

Find ways to appeal to both. For those that are thriving in the work from home environment (often employees with kids or those who have long commutes), embrace the flexibility that's allowing them to find work-life balance. Turn 1:1 meetings into "walk and talks" so they can get their exercise while also having the conversations that need to be had. For the other 21% (often single employees or empty nesters), they're probably craving community, so it's important to find ways to provide meaningful connection to simulate an office environment (see the next tip!).

10. Offer support to manage employee burnout.

To combat burnout, Apeel made it a company-wide objective to implement "thoughtful investment in the whole employee—focusing on wellness and restorative programs," says Megan. The underlying KRs included things like

(*continued*)

[3]Nicholas Bloom, "Don't Let Employees Pick Their WFH Days," *Harvard Business Review*, May 25, 2021, https://hbr.org/2021/05/dont-let-employees-pick-their-wfh-days.

monthly wellness campaigns and other smaller initiatives to prioritize health.

Pro tip: Add wellness-focused objectives into your OKR mix next quarter.

Unbounce similarly prioritized wellness over the past year. They gave all employees access to Headspace, an app that promotes meditation and mindfulness, in addition to a $500 health and wellness allowance. They also hosted virtual gardening, cooking, and art classes to bring people—especially those who have been living alone during the pandemic—together in ways that feel natural.

11. Double down in employee burnout best practices.

It's easy to slip away from best practices in a remote workplace, and yet, it's more important than ever to double down on them. Stacey witnessed this at her organization, as managers began to revert to behaviors that didn't align with the leadership style she knew they were capable of.

To combat this, she reminds her leaders to manage through performance, not the "green dot."

If your employees are hitting the mark, stop obsessing over whether they're available on Slack or Teams when you are—encourage that mid-day walk, workout block on the calendar, or whatever else you know lights your employees up. Focus on employee impact, not time spent at the desk.

Sample OKRs for the HR Team

OKR Examples for Human Resource Leadership

- **Objective:** Ensure our employees come to work happy and engaged.

- **Key Results**
  - Increase employee satisfaction survey score average from 75% to 90%.
  - 90% of our employees attend four or five courses for internal career development.
  - Increase percentage of exit interviews from 50% to 90%.
- **Key Initiatives:**
  - Increase internal job mobility for our employees.
  - Conduct interviews to collect top reasons for turnover.
- **Objective:** Develop a comprehensive diversity and inclusion program.
- **Key Results**
  - 80% of our employees rate our DEI efforts as good to better.
  - Increase retention rate by 10% for all minority groups.
  - 90% of our employees participate in our ERF community at least once a month.
  - Increase company diversity from 20% to 30% to better reflect the local community we serve.
- **Key Initiatives:**
  - Create a DEI council.
  - Empower all employees to take part in monthly DEI sessions.
- **Objective:** Create and launch a modern employee hiring portal on our website.
- **Key Results**
  - Increase visits to portal by 25% month-over-month.
  - Reduce number of steps to submit applications from 3 to 1.
  - Reduce the time to publish new job postings live on the website from 5 days to 24 hours.
- **Key Initiative:**
  - Develop staging site for stakeholder review.

- **Objective:** Build a goal-setting culture by implementing an OKR program across the company.
- **Key Results**
  - Conduct 12 weekly training sessions to onboard and educate new employees about OKR best practices.
  - 80% of employees are performing weekly check-ins.
  - Reduce department-level OKR review and preparation time from 14 days to 5 days.
  - 90% of employees rate transparency and accountability as high post-OKR implementation.
- **Key Initiatives:**
  - Establish OKR champions for each department.
  - Implement OKR software.

The Sales Team

From increasing revenue to building loyal customer relationships, the sales team plays a significant role in driving overall business growth. Yet this department highlights a critical challenge when it comes to the OKR framework: How do you establish stretch goals that motivate, when quotas are well-defined and tied to compensation? In this section, I address the difference between OKRs and quotas, how to adapt, and, most importantly, discuss why OKRs help in fostering engagement and transparency across a sales organization, which leads to better work culture, productivity, and, ultimately, stronger outcomes.

OKR Benefits for the Sales Team

Most sales teams are focused on quotas—individual goals, specifically tied to hitting a revenue target. But the strongest sales leaders know that much more goes into developing a scalable sales program built for long-term success. If quotas are all you and your team focus on, you'll lose sight of other key investments you need to make to achieve sustainable and continued growth.

In general, I've found that sales leaders are most successful when they have a healthy mix of stretch targets for the team, and committed OKRs that map to quotas. We recommend a stretch target that is 20-30% higher than the team quota. This encourages the teams and each rep to get creative about how they work together to stretch and think bigger than the minimum bar, while there also is an additional model behind the scenes that takes compensation into account.

OKRs help sales teams stay focused on the right initiatives and drive long-term pipeline by:

- **Promoting engagement:** Sales OKRs provide a sense of belonging and purpose to a sales team, connecting account executives, sales development, enablement, and every other member of the team to a common purpose. Camaraderie is important when building a motivated sales team.

- **Clarifying roles and adding transparency:** OKRs provide transparency and clarify the role of each person on the team when it comes to achieving the objective at hand. Sales teams often feel the most siloed, because their work is often done on the phone with prospects, or on the road meeting clients. OKRs also provide context into the broader business, as documenting progress lets everyone know what's happening across different departments.

- **Offering long-term focus:** OKRs help focus sales teams on achieving the business outcomes and building long-term customer relationships rather than focusing only on reaching the sales quotas.

Challenges and How to Address Them

Sales leaders are used to adapting when unforeseen changes happen. But one of the ways they develop that ability is by preparing for every scenario possible. When implementing an OKR practice, you can expect challenges that are specific to sales departments.

> **Challenge:** A common hurdle that I've heard from countless organizations is that members of the sales team are concerned that OKRs will become yet another metric tracked against their compensation.
>
> **Solution:** As a part of your rollout, be intentional about the OKR training you provide the sales team so they understand why you are rolling out OKRs and how OKRs and quotas will work together in your particular sales organization. The goal is to enable accountability, collaboration, and a connection to positive business outcomes, not to introduce a new way to measure individual compensation.
>
> **Challenge:** Sales teams spend the majority of their time trying to achieve their quotas. Initiatives that ladder up to overarching objectives but aren't directly tied to the quota are hard to understand, communicate, and prioritize.
>
> **Solution:** Create cross-departmental syncs with other leaders, to discuss how their own OKRs connect to company revenue. This will make the steel thread clearer to your sales team and how they should think about their own contributions, as well as create a more creative and collaborative approach to their sales motion. I'd also recommend that sales teams not *only* structure their OKRs around revenue.

There are many other areas you will want to capture in your department OKRs. These OKRs are critical to the longevity of your sales reps. Focus on behavioral changes and consider building objectives around process management, a better team spirit, or improved cross-functional collaboration.

How to Connect OKRs to Sales Team Rhythms and Tools

Sales leadership involves more repetition than many other roles. In order to be successful, a sales rep needs to be able to replicate success. Which talk track, email cadence, or pitch process worked to close the most business? How can I make an impact on the overall business?

Answering these questions starts with coaching. I am not a sales leader. As a serial founder, I've developed a strong understanding of the sales process, but I'm not an inherent sales trainer. To bridge that gap, I asked Amanda Gates from People Stretch Solutions to share her thoughts on the topic.

Before I turn it over to Amanda, though, I want to share one piece of advice as a business leader. Track your sales metrics, quotas, and velocity alongside your sales team's OKR progress. Whether you use software, spreadsheets, or a whiteboard, this will give both you and your team the full picture, and give your broader leadership team the context they need to review both sets of metrics. Ideally, you use this to frame your weekly and monthly team meetings.

> ## It Starts with Coaching
>
> *Amanda Gates, People Stretch Solutions*
>
> Everyone has some level of awareness around the importance of setting goals, and many know how to set goals. Yet, goal-setting is a skill set that few companies develop to the point of

(*continued*)

competency. For businesses, the lack of effective goal-setting is not just an innocent character flaw of sales managers—it's a critical deficiency that can define the difference between hitting your revenue expectations and hitting a wall.

While it may sound like a paranoid hot take, goal-setting is a skill that can have a significant effect on you, your sales team, and your company's bottom line. As a critical first step within the coaching process, goal-setting skills are in sales teams managed by a strong coach. And that is precisely where things start to fall apart: there are very few sales managers who invest in their coaching skills, and this unfortunate piece of data leads to a host of troubling statistics. For example, more than 60% of sales professionals will leave the team if they do not have a good coach, and that number may include your star performer!

But that is just one of several severe consequences of an underdeveloped coaching cadence:

1. Failure to hit the sales number for a given quarter or even for the year
2. Inability to set clear expectations and hold people accountable

Tie Individual Goals to Organizational Strategy

A quick self-analysis can help you determine if your sales department could benefit from a regular cadence of role-play activities:

1. How many opportunities are lost because your team was not prepared?
2. What methods, if any, do you have to prepare salespeople for an important client meeting?

3. Are your salespeople overconfident about their customer meeting skills?

4. Do your salespeople position their questions in a way to get the most information?

5. Do your team members have shy, insecure body language?

Many sales professionals think their sales skills are so strong that they can "wing it" when it comes to meetings with clients. Salespeople frequently will say, "I have been doing this for a long time. Nobody can rattle me." The only thing this proves is that they are overconfident and maybe even insecure.

In no other profession would this be an acceptable attitude; a doctor or lawyer would not walk into a meeting largely unprepared, basing their actions on a "gut feeling" coming from the confidence of experience! Why are salespeople not held to a higher standard of training and preparation? It is an excellent and somewhat befuddling question.

Assess Your Coaching Skills to Address the Issue

Addressing the issue by assessing your coaching skills can put your entire sales organization on the path toward reaching their sales goals:

1. Sales managers can improve the performance of a sales team through goal-setting, which is part of the coaching skillset.

2. The end of the quarter is an ideal time for sales managers to set coaching goals for themselves and schedule goal-setting activities for their teams.

(*continued*)

3. Structured, regular coaching by the sales manager around goals—company, team, and individual goals—supports the desire and commitment of the entire sales team, which is fundamental to sustainable success in sales.

When it comes to sales, effective coaching is absolutely necessary to see the performance you desire. Starting with goal-setting lets you and the sales rep structure a plan for success while making them aware of how their work impacts the organization's strategic objectives—not just revenue.

Sales Alignment

When business environments become tumultuous, they often take with them those ambitious goals your sales managers, sales reps, and sales enablement teams have shared with you. Asking employees to create and share their mission and initiatives is only the first step in effective coaching around goals. Once that information is available, individual goals must be aligned to the overall company strategy and mission to generate the most powerful tool for carrying action forward and sustaining momentum.

Individual goal-setting is an essential first step, but without goal alignment, this information will not drive revenue growth, for several reasons. First, a collection of personal goals that do not coalesce into a larger one may result in people moving in different directions. Second, sales managers cannot communicate something they do not know, and must first be clear on company goals before being able to align employee goals.

When sales managers are clear on the team's individual goals and the company's strategic goals, they can find the intersection between these sets of goals. Alignment occurs when the manager gets buy-in from the team and can frequently reference these goals as part of their coaching routine. We find that unfamiliarity with coaching cadence and lack of coaching skills often prevents sales managers from following up with goal alignment.

Effective goal alignment can have a significant impact on revenue:

- It improves and accelerates operational execution as teams move quickly from strategy planning to execution.

- It creates ownership in the organization's success, resulting in more engaged employees and increased retention rates.

- It reduces or eliminates time wasted on unrelated tasks due to communicated and aligned goals.

- It provides sustainable motivation and momentum by minimizing the "roller coaster" of inevitable sales ups and downs as managers weave individual goals into the coaching process.

Goal Alignment Is Critical to Maintaining Momentum

Statistics show that 40% of results happen in the last one-third of the program. This reinforces the goal gradient theory, which says the closer people get to the goal, the more effort they put into achieving it.

Goal alignment enables management to make strategic decisions quickly. Since teams will already be working on the most critical initiatives, changes can be made on the fly; this reduces the time wasted by confusion over objectives or conflicting priorities.

(continued)

Goal Alignment Results in More Engaged and Focused Employees Who Won't Leave Their Jobs

Goal alignment is a useful tool to communicate expectations, document progress, and identify employee strengths and weaknesses. When employees understand the company's mission and how their contribution impacts that mission, real organizational success is possible.

Tapping into the intrinsic motivation of a person is the most powerful tool you can have as a sales manager. Know what makes your people tick in terms of career goals or personal goals (within reason). Coaching provides an excellent tool for asking the right questions to get at the heart of a person's intentions.

But knowing the company mission and the goals of an individual are of little strategic value without finding a way to align them. The genius of an effective sales manager is their ability to align overarching company objectives to the sales rep's individual goals. It establishes a "want to" versus a "have to" outlook for the sales team. If the manager has excelled in aligning personal career goals with organizational goals, they make it much easier for their individual sales team members to take ownership of the goals and move toward them with a greater sense of accountability.

It's All About What Drives Revenue

As a manager, your sales reps' energy to drive toward a revenue goal is one of your most renewable resources. Consider that it is challenging for sales professionals to sell when they are not engaged, but it can seem effortless when they engage with a well-aligned goal; that intersection where the individual's *why* meets the organizational *why*. Consistently bringing coaching conversations back to goals—the professional and personal *why*—can redirect attention, reduce distractions, and provide an energy boost to get the job done.

Sample OKRs for the Sales Team

OKR Examples for Sales Leadership

- **Objective:** Drive record-breaking growth in Q4 to increase financial stability.
- **Key Results**
  - Generate $3.5 million in new mid-enterprise sales pipeline.
  - Reduce closed/lost opportunities from 100 to 25.
  - Increase weekly demo bookings from 20 to 50.
- **Key Initiatives:**
  - Run sales plays in new market.
  - Hire four new AEs.
  - Reduce closed/lost opportunities.
- **Objective:** Streamline sales pipeline in order to help our AEs work more efficiently.
- **Key Results**
  - Reduce sales cycle from 35 to 24 days.
  - Increase quota attainment by rep from 60% to 78%.
  - Increase SQL win rate from 40% to 56%.
- **Key Initiatives:**
  - Objection handling workshop for all AEs.
  - New sales deck focused on value instead of features.
- **Objective:** Achieve record sales in our new customer growth segment.

- **Key Results**
  - Close $500,000 in new enterprise (ENT) deals.
  - Close $300,000 in new mid-market (MM) deals.
  - Close $200,000 in new small and medium-sized business (SMB) deals.
- **Key Initiatives:**
  - Establish upsell plans for each segment.
  - Build product adoption triggers for each segment.
- **Objective:** Move to a territory-focused sales model.
- **Key Results**
  - 100% of AEs have completed their territory strategy presentation.
  - Leads per territory are within 20% variance.
- **Key Initiatives:**
  - Establish new territory model and comp plans.
  - Pair AEs and SDRs based on territory.

OKR Examples for Sales Development Teams

- **Objective:** Improve inbound lead processing.
- **Key Results**
  - Answer all website inquiries from within 20 hours to within 16 hours.
  - Administer 92% of all inbound demo requests from within 36 hours to within 24 hours.
  - Reduce on-page chat response time from 120 seconds to less than 90 seconds.
  - Increase weekly demo booking by 12%.

- **Key Initiatives:**
  - Build new response sequences for all demo requests from new markets.
  - Create SDR on-call schedule.
- **Objective:** Improve prospect qualification process.
- **Key Results**
  - Increase number of inbound leads reaching discovery stage in 5 days from 38% to 48%.
  - Book 150 prospect meetings.
  - Generate $250,000 in sales opportunities.
  - Increase percentage of second conversations from 25% to 35%.
- **Key Initiatives:**
  - Audit all unaccepted sales prospects to determine why they didn't meet criteria.
  - Implement lead enrichment tool.
- **Objective:** Amplify effectiveness of outbound sales development strategy.
- **Key Results**
  - Touch 125 unique accounts.
  - Contact 300 MQLs.
  - Improve average call length from 4 minutes to 6+ minutes.
  - Increase outbound pursuit duration from 20 days to 27 days.
- **Key Initiatives:**
  - Develop new SDR outbound script.
  - Launch ABM campaign for key industries.

OKR Examples for Account Executives (AEs)

- **Objective:** Increase reach and engagement of key stakeholders inside target accounts.

- **Key Results**
  - Increase cold calls from 20 to 25 per day.
  - Increase intro emails sent from 20 to 25 per day.
  - Increase discovery meetings completed from 3 to 5 per week.
  - Increase conversion rate of outbound meetings into opportunities from 20% to 25%.
- **Key Initiative:**
  - Define key target account list for each AE.
- **Objective:** Accelerate inbound sales process.
- **Key Results**
  - Reduce response time for all new sales inquiries from within 5 hours to within 2 hours.
  - Shorten average time from inquiry to demo from 48 hours to 36 hours.
  - Decrease average time from proposal to decision from 5 days to 3 days.
  - Increase deals closed from 7 to 10 this quarter.
- **Key Initiative:**
  - Redefine discovery "Q&A."

The Marketing Team

Marketing is a unique department, because the focuses and functions of each team member are very specific and distinct from one another. While a sales or engineering team has groups of people doing essentially the same type of work, a marketing team will often include growth marketers, campaign managers, product marketers, content marketers, designers, videographers, and more. OKRs bring each of those disparate roles together with common purpose in mind, and a shared understanding of how each function will contribute.

OKR Benefits for the Marketing Team

OKRs provide many benefits to marketing teams. In a function that is a combination of both quantitative and qualitative work, OKRs bring a focused clarity to the work that spans both. The following are several benefits I've found marketing teams gain from leveraging the OKR framework.

1. **Focus:** Without well-defined objectives, marketing becomes a game of trying to hit a moving target. OKRs focus efforts, but, when activated intentionally, they also capture the "soft" marketing work of brand-building, thought leadership, and content quality that traditional revenue-focused KPIs can miss but are critical for long-term success.

2. **Aligning Functions:** With so many distinct aspects to marketing and so many varied outcomes of campaigns and strategies, marketing OKRs can assist in achieving the results you want by aligning and focusing efforts around the most impactful outcomes the team can drive, together.

3. **Shift from Outputs to Outcomes:** OKRs provide a mindset shift from tactics to business outcomes, which can be a necessary change for a production-minded team.

Challenges and How to Address Them

Challenge: Marketing teams often have metrics tracked not only for broader brand awareness and engagement, but also for revenue metrics lower down the funnel. Teams often split these into separate parts of the business and end up working in silos, with many pieces of a large puzzle affecting similar results.

Solution: By establishing a marketing-wide set of objectives, teams will focus their efforts to be complementary, and duplicative work will be addressed in the planning process, instead of later on as a surprise. This will be a forcing function for owners of specific metrics to align the work done to drive those metrics to one another.

Challenge: It's easy to spin up a new campaign within a bubble. The challenge is trying to figure out how each campaign ladders up to the overarching purpose.

Solution: With OKRs, the starting point is the business objective you're trying to reach. So each campaign will be built to support that purpose.

How to Connect to Department-Specific Rhythms and Tools

A common issue many businesses run into is the relationship between sales and marketing. Marketing has a broad set of responsibilities, but, in many cases, those are second to one thing: driving revenue production. To dig in on this relationship, I turned to a marketing leader—and one of his sales counterparts—I've worked with.

Stop Fighting Over the Funnel

Kevin Shively, serial marketing leader

You have never heard a sales leader come to a marketing leader and say, "We need to talk about our brand's Twitter engagement."

In general, marketing fails when it isn't aligned with sales. Marketing programs are successful when the sales team is successful, when our customers are successful, or when our product's features are adopted.

Even still, most marketing goals and objectives are developed in a silo.

I've managed OKRs for marketing teams at three companies now, and one of the biggest mistakes I've seen made—and made myself—is not partnering with other departments to create alignment as we set our objectives, priorities, and commitments.

In this post, I'll share some OKR examples that will keep your sales and marketing teams connected, but first I want to share three reasons *why* it matters, and I've brought our VP of sales, Chris Pitchford, to help.

Three Reasons to Build Marketing and Sales Goals Together

1. The customer experience

As a marketer, it's easy to think only in terms of metrics: visits, leads, conversion rates, revenue, etc. But the top mandate for a marketer needs to be thinking like a human. The same is true for sales. Volume means nothing if we're not considering the experience of the customer (who, believe it or not, is also a human).

"It's easy to build programs that continuously increase touch points; you just add another email or phone call," says Pitchford. "But when we don't coordinate efforts, that gets overwhelming for the person evaluating our product or service, and our effort works against us. We have to consider the customer's experience, first and foremost, or no one wins."

(continued)

2. The funnel breaks

As a marketer, the sales team's forecast is reliant on the marketing forecast. If marketing is focused on Offer X, which has a closed/won rate of Y%, and sales is building goals based on the understanding that marketing is driving Offer Q, which has a closed/won rate of Z%, that misalignment can be costly. It influences focus, tactics, talk tracks, and staffing. Conversely, marketing needs to know what sales capacity and requirements are in order to know where they need to double down.

"One of marketing's primary jobs is to find new leads and new ways to qualify and get them sales-ready," says Pitchford. "But that requires testing and changing things, which can impact pipeline volume and velocity. The two teams need to be in lockstep about what the goals and commitments are in order to do this in a sustainable and scalable way."

3. The feedback loop breaks

As a marketer, you should spend most of your time thinking about the customer and what they want, need, etc. How did that message resonate? How did it miss? What do we need to do differently? The sales process is an extension of your messaging and your greatest resource when it comes to understanding what is working, but if you're pointing in different directions, there will be a misalignment and a gap in understanding.

"My team is on the phone, interacting via email and chat, and listening to the needs and concerns of the market every day," says Pitchford. "We have the best pulse on why people buy, and why they don't, which is a critical piece of feedback for marketing."

How to Build Marketing OKRs That Sales Will Love

Creating OKRs for a marketing team can be tricky. It's easy to focus on tactics, since the tactics that influence these OKRs are where the real magic happens, but remember that your objectives should be ambitious, and the key results should be measurable and impactful.

It's also important to avoid vanity metrics as key results. Think in terms of winning the objective; "If I achieve all of these key results, will I have hit the objective?" Once these are defined, the tactics can be built to drive each key result.

Below are some sample OKRs for aligning marketing to sales goals. Each of these objectives focuses on a different component of the marketing-sales motion: driving quality leads, facilitating sales-readiness, discovering growth levers, enabling the sales motion, and increasing velocity and conversion rates.

Objective: Drive qualified leads for the sales team.

Key Result (Volume): Drive XX SALs.

Key Initiative (Quality): Increase MQL:SQL conversion rate.

Key Result (Growth): Drive 10% of SALs from new channels.

(continued)

Objective: Become the most recognized brand in our industry.

Key Initiative: Run XX partner marketing programs to expose ourselves to new audiences.

Key Result: Generate XX press mentions through contributed articles.

Key Result: Advertise in XX industry trade publications.

Objective: Build capacity to scale.

Key Initiative: Establish a referral program that drives XX new leads in-period.

Key Result: Book XX meetings from organic channels.

Key Result: Drive XX top-of-funnel leads via content promotion.

Objective: Arm sales team with "wow-worthy" collateral.

Key Result (Volume): Deliver XX pieces of sales-accepted collateral.

Key Result (Quality): Marketing collateral used to assist XX% of sales conversations.

Key Initiative (Differentiation): New messaging and positioning is reflected in XX/XX pieces of sales collateral.

Objective: Improve funnel mechanics to deliver XX sales-ready leads.

Key Initiative: Audit all prospect touch points to increase conversion rate at 3/4 sales stages.

Key Result: Create programmatic approach to lead quality loss analysis of 100% of lost deals.

Key Result: Increase sales velocity among key ICPs by XX%.

I hope these examples are helpful starters, but I want to remind you that you shouldn't just copy and paste these. Each business is different, and your marketing OKRs should be developed hand-in-hand with your sales leaders.

Sample OKRs for the Marketing Team

OKR Examples for Marketing Leadership   Marketing leaders are responsible for the overall marketing plan and strategy. Their world is comprised of product marketing, digital programs, communications, campaigns, and more. It's important for marketing leaders to design goals that set the stage for the rest of the marketing department.

- **Objective:** Improve end-to-end process to improve closing rate.
- **Key Results**
  - Acquire 9,500 new qualified leads for sales by Q1.
  - Drive $100 million in marketing-generated pipeline by Q1.
  - Create four top-of-funnel pieces of collateral for sales by end of Q1.
- **Key Initiatives:**
  - Execute targeted lead campaign.
  - Sponsor major industry event.

OKR Examples for Demand Generation

- **Objective:** Strengthen brand as leader in space to increase monthly website visitors.
- **Key Results**
  - Increase our organic unique visitors by 25%.
  - Grow social media followers from 50,000 to 75,000.
  - Boost NPS score from 7 to 8.
- **Key Initiatives:**
  - A/B test messaging and ad creative on key channels.
  - Increase enterprise customer video testimonials from 5 to 7 QoQ.
- **Objective:** Achieve record-breaking marketing engagement to increase paying customers.
- **Key Results**
  - Generate 60,000 unique website visitors in Q3.
  - Obtain 4,000 new trial signups in Q3.
  - Convert 1,400 new paid customers in Q3.
- **Key Initiative:**
  - Build new demo nurture sequence that maps to topline campaigns and audience.

OKR Examples for Marketing Events

- **Objective:** Drive record ROI from marketing events.
- **Key Results**
  - Scan 1,200 badges during event.
  - Book 10 on-site sales meetings during event.
  - Generate $370,000 in sales pipeline from event in Q2.
  - Achieve 13% post-show engagement from attendees.

- **Key Initiative:**
  - Sponsor world-class event.

OKR Examples for Content Marketing

- **Objective:** Create top tier content to increase reach of product launch.
- **Key Results**
  - Increase our organic web traffic by 500K UVs.
  - Write 12 blog posts.
  - Increase our social media impressions by 1 million.
- **Key Initiatives:**
  - Build and stick to editorial calendar.
  - Write two top-of-funnel marketing pieces.

OKR Examples for Marketing Ops

- **Objective:** Implement the best email marketing software for the business to engage more prospects.
- **Key Results**
  - Book 50 prospect meetings via email marketing campaign.
- **Key Initiatives:**
  - Complete Marketing Automation certification.
  - Launch email marketing software by EOQ.
  - Drive 150 leads through email marketing campaign.

OKR Examples for Product Marketing

- **Objective:** Create the best customer advisory board experience.

- **Key Results**
  - Drive 50 customer executives to participate in quarterly meeting.
  - Curate top 10 customer pain points.
  - Facilitate post-meeting follow up with plan to address top three business issues.
  - Receive 90% satisfaction rate on post-meeting survey.
- **Key Initiative:**
  - Build Customer Advisory meeting syllabus and content.
- **Objective:** Become customer-obsessed and understand voice of customer to increase retention.
- **Key Results**
  - Conduct 20 in-depth interviews with existing and churned customers.
  - Listen to 50 sales calls.
  - Conduct survey of customer satisfaction with minimum of 2,000 users.
  - Create list of top 10 customer challenges and share with product team.
- **Key Initiative:**
  - Develop meeting cadence with sales and CX teams to understand core needs.
- **Objective:** Elevate customer engagement program.
- **Key Results**
  - Increase customer engagement via email and in-app messages from 20% to 30%.
  - Create self-service customer academy with 12 modules full of videos and documentation.
  - Reduce Tier 1 support requests from 100 to 50 by promoting new self-service academy.

- **Key Initiative:**
  - Build customer community platform.

OKR Examples for Brand Awareness

- **Objective:** Elevate the company brand to increase awareness and engagement to ultimately increase trial signups.
- **Key Results**
  - Increase trial signups by 25%.
  - Increase media placements QoQ from 5 to 10.
  - Optimize blog to rank for five specific search terms to increase organic traffic by 25% QoQ.
- **Key Initiative:**
  - Launch thought leadership campaign.

The Customer Success Team

The customer success team is responsible for ensuring success of and satisfaction with your product or service. On top of that, this department generally fields support requests and is the first line of defense for frustration and potential churn. The attention to detail that is necessary for a customer success team is critical, and a success leader's ability to understand how their team is doing against their goals can be a leading indicator of how the customer is doing.

OKR Benefits for the Success Team

There are several benefits that the OKR framework brings to customer success teams.

1. **Continuous Improvement:** OKRs offer a framework to track progress period over period at the team level, which

allows both the entire group and each individual contributor to scale and improve the implementation and adoption process for every customer.

2. **Topline Focus:** Often, customer success metrics are ignored at the leadership level, where new business metrics are front and center. For a business to be sustainable, customer satisfaction, retention, and expansion need to be top of mind for the entire business, because this can impact product decisions, marketing plans, forecasting, sales strategy, and the direction of the business as a whole. The OKR framework brings these core metrics into the most important conversations taking place across the business.

How to Connect to Department-Specific Rhythms and Tools

While customer success teams have a unique challenge in that they need to align to every part of the business in order to perform their primary function successfully, they also have a unique challenge in that they're responsible for the business's most valuable asset: its customer's happiness. This focuses the various customer success functions in different ways, and those can sometimes be at odds. To gain an insider's perspective of how to create unified customer experience goals, I turned to a longtime success leader I've worked with.

Why Unified Customer Experience Goals Are the Future (and How to Set Them)

Jenny Lindstein, enterprise customer success leader

Whether you work in software or retail, your peers are now putting their customers at the center of their goals and objectives by identifying simple key strategic initiatives that every team can now align to and support.

Examples of unified customer experience goals include "Deliver an exceptional customer experience to our in-store customers" and "Ensure next-day shipping for all orders placed online." These goals can also include increasing customer sentiment (NPS), increasing lifetime value (LTV), and increasing average order size (AOV) or lifetime value (LTV) as key focus areas for the company quarter after quarter and year after year.

These customer-focused, top-level goals for customer experience align teams around a collective mission instead of siloed department metrics and revenue goals.

Examples of Customer Experience Goals

Let's take a customer-centered goal of "Increase customer AOV by 10% this year." Typically, there may be a small team working on this strategic initiative already, fighting for resources and focus from different teams in order to move the needle—oftentimes, unsuccessfully.

But by setting this customer-centered goal at the top level across all customer experience teams, every team can focus their efforts (and teams) on supporting the mission— and, more importantly, understand how the work they're doing on a daily basis ladders up to this business imperative.

- For brand teams, this might mean moving their content and awareness strategy away from pushing single product education across different channels to focusing on content that packages many different products together at once; for example, pushing a complete

(*continued*)

look from top to bottom versus a single pair of shoes. Or, alternatively, shifting focus to highlighting premium products that come with higher price tags instead of their lower-tier lines.

- For e-commerce teams this might mean optimizing the company's website to display recommended and suggested items on each product page to increase average cart sizes or bundling items on the website to encourage purchasing more items at once for a discount. To support the customer goal in this case, this team might shift their focus from new web projects they had planned to simply improving and optimizing the current pages they already have today.

- For customer support teams this might mean sacrificing a few percentage points on average handle time in order to spend more time on the phone with VIP customers to chat them through new items that have just arrived that they know they will love based on their purchase history with the brand. To support the customer goal in this case, this team would expand their focus from not just being reactive to service requests but to becoming a proactive strategic upselling arm for the company.

In the cases above, when your customer experience goals are aligned around the customer problem you are trying to solve versus department-specific metrics, all teams involved in the customer journey can rethink their departmental strategies to directly impact the business objectives.

The key here is understanding that by bringing this customer focus across teams you are oftentimes deprioritizing the importance of something else, and that's okay! The retailers that focus on a few key customer initiatives quarter by quarter are the ones that in the end are providing the best experience for their customers, keeping customers happy, and, most importantly, coming back for more.

Here's a sample of customer experience OKRs that work for several major retail organizations.

Objectives (O)	Key Results (KRs)	Key Initiatives (KIs)
Loyalty program—Develop an attractive loyalty program to improve customer retention.	• Percentage of customers availing loyalty programs to increase from 8% to 15%. • Targeted communication to customers to drive points redemption in online channel—from 5,000 to 10,000.	• Develop a program to deliver seamless loyalty redemption across online and offline channels.
One view of customer—Capture entire customer journey and have one view of the customer to deliver better customer experience.	• Increase the number of key customer details captured in online channel from four to eight for better targeting. • Capture at least five data points on customers in offline stores. • Gather feedback of 100 customers across online and offline channels each to capture the customer journey.	• Develop a program to deliver seamless loyalty points redemption across online and offline channels. • Develop a customer data capture mechanism/ process for offline stores. • Survey rollout in offline and online channels.

(continued)

Wow the customers with an incredible in-store digital experience.	• Institutionalize three digital interventions (endless aisles, pricing displays, digital product catalog) across 10 stores that will create customer delight. • 15% of the customers walking into the store engaged with digital experience.	• Identify vendors and roll-out plan for digital interventions within stores.

Deploying a Customer Experience Goal Framework

For retailers looking to bring all their customer experience teams together to focus on the most important business priorities, the OKR (objectives and key results) goal management framework is a tried-and-true approach.

Step 1: Align Your Customer Experience Teams

Get in the same virtual or "real world" room. Explain the "why" behind coming up with unified customer experience goals: to align yourselves around the same key customer experience metrics so you're marching to the beat of the same drum—doing what's best for the customer and, ultimately, your own individual department goals by ensuring laser-focused alignment.

- Move away from silo team planning to have everyone align around common goals centered on your customer experience.
- When everyone is aligned around the output of happy, loyal customers, every team wins.

- Ditch tactical department-level tracking to stay focused on key customer metrics that push the business forward.

Step 2: Come Up with Your OKRs Together

Use the objective key results framework to come up with your OKRs together across team leadership. Remember, your objective is the goal you are all aligning around, such as "Become the #1 market leader in the North American region." Your key results are the specific, measurable steps all teams involved will take to achieve that objective. If each functional group within the customer experience journey can break customer-centered goals down to each of their team members, everyone becomes accountable for a small customer experience metric output that leads to huge team wins in the aggregate.

Step 3: Commit to Transparent Communication, Tracking, and Updates

Goal-setting doesn't get you anywhere if you're not checking in on progress. Keep team meetings and 1:1s focused around progress to goals, not around-the-room updates. This will create one source of truth for your goal tracking, allowing you to know at all times where you're on track and where you're falling behind.

It's time to move away from manual goal tracking. Goal tracking for the customer experience journey doesn't have to be an ongoing manual burden. There may be hesitancy to implement the OKR framework with hundreds of supporting employees who don't need an extra burden. With OKR software, your employees don't have to lift a finger.

(*continued*)

- Integrate into all your key systems (marketing and customer service systems) so you never have to manually give goal updates and have real-time access to goal progress.

- Automatically track toward goals to know where you are falling short and need to invest more resources or training.

However you implement your OKR framework, if you do it with a thoughtful approach and intentional rollout, you'll give your teams the focus, clarity, and transparency they need to be successful.

OKR Examples for Customer Success Leadership

- **Objective:** Scale and improve implementation and adoption process for managed customers.
- **Key Results**
  - 90% of all customers live in four weeks.
  - 90% of customers reach their engagement threshold within two weeks of going live.
- **Key Initiatives:**
  - Launch weekly standup program with CX team.
  - Establish milestones for engagement.
- **Objective:** Increase existing customer expansion revenue.
- **Key Results**
  - Increase revenue from $1 million to $2 million.
  - Increase amount of quarterly business reviews conducted from 75% to 90%.

- 100% of contract renewal reports are delivered to customer success 60 days in advance.
- **Key Initiative:**
- Develop sales partnership plan.
- **Objective:** Drive customer subscriptions up.
- **Key Results**
- Increase annual customer subscriptions by 10%.
- Increase subscription profit margins by 5%.
- Maintain a cancellation level of less than 5%.
- **Key Initiative:**
- Simplify subscription process with Operations department.
- **Objective:** Deliver exceptional customer service through client support and education.
- **Key Results**
- Reduce support phone call abandonment rate from 14% to 9%.
- Decrease average speed to problem resolution from three days to one day.
- Monitor and update automated chatbot responses to increase problem resolution rate from 38% to 50%.
- Increase baseline satisfaction rate for customer support and training team from 81% to 90%.
- Update and refresh onboarding education curriculum to drive more efficient product adoption.
- **Key Initiatives:**
- Build customer education portal.
- Customer support training program.

Running the Business with OKRs

The ability to structure, define, and align your OKRs is the first part of the equation. OKRs are intended to be a catalyst for powerful conversations, and those conversations need to happen on a regular basis. This is where so many companies fail to implement OKRs effectively. In order for OKRs to stick, and stick for everyone, they need to be central to how you operate and how you execute.

Part III provides a detailed playbook outlining the cadence and rhythms that will keep your business moving forward by leveraging your OKRs.

Remember that the preceding blueprint and the following guide are designed to create a system that makes OKRs stick.

Without the right cadence and rhythms, your OKRs will not have the high impact they can.

If you're an executive leader reading this, my hope is that it will be a valuable guide to how you can foster and cultivate a culture of transparency, focus, agility, and continuous learning using OKRs. If you're a departmental or team manager, this will help create the systems by which your team operates with a deep sense of purpose and focus on the top priorities.

15

Expect and Prepare
for a Challenge

I recently spoke with Derek, who works for a major technology company. OKRs had been rolled out across Derek's division of the organization, and everyone was excited. Then, the team quickly realized that they weren't going to have what they needed to be successful, but would still be held accountable for their adoption of the process. Derek was brand-new to the OKR process, and already disappointed in its extra work and clear lack of direction.

I can't count the number of customers we've worked with who reached out because they'd tried to roll out OKRs and had a bit of a rough time for the first couple of quarters. In most cases, my team was able to work with them to uncover the issues plaguing OKR adoption, the subsequent quarter got easier, and, finally, OKR adoption became a natural part of their business rhythm.

Don't lose the excitement as you embark on this journey, but do expect that, like anything else in life, the rollout of this framework will ebb and flow.

OKR Rhythm Fundamentals:
The Three Cs: Create, Check-In, Close

At a high level, the best way to think about OKR rhythms is that they include time to plan, time to execute, and time to reflect. I encourage businesses to invest time and effort into the 3Cs: create, check-in, and close.

To ensure high adoption of your OKR program, implement the 3Cs from the start and consistently follow this rhythm with each planning cycle. Show this visual when rolling out OKRs to your leaders so they can see how all these pieces come together.

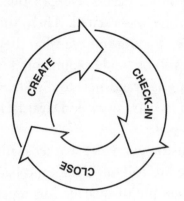

Create: Before each quarter

✓ Department OKRs are defined based on the company's annual OKRs.

✓ Team and individual OKRs created and aligned.

Check-in: Throughout the quarter

✓ Evaluate your OKR progress and discuss evaluation within senior management.

✓ Address at-risk or off-track OKRs and course-correct where possible.

Close: At end of quarter

✓ Score and close OKRs in your software solution.

✓ Conduct retrospectives and team rituals to learn from wins and losses, and carry into next quarter.

OKRs in the Real World: Josh Hug and Remitly's Quarterly Stake in the Ground

For Josh Hug, COO and co-founder of Remitly, the company's OKR journey and maturity evolved as the company grew.

Early on, leadership would set annual goals and then do two-week company sprints. They quickly started to scale beyond that, however, and started to separate different teams and started to establish monthly goals, eventually leading to setting quarterly goals.

"What we found was that our team felt like we were changing the goals more rapidly. We didn't have as much stability in goal setting, even though, from our perspective, we had some annual goals that we rarely changed . . . but we would change our focus on a quarterly basis and that became disruptive," Hug said. "That's when we decided to land on OKRs, because we felt like it created a framework to allow for permission for the team to recognize that they have a set quarterly goal and that they're going to change it on a quarterly basis."

Hug said their teams manage their goal check-ins and that they have autonomy in how they do that.

At the company level, Hug said they go through a pretty rigorous process to set quarterly goals.

"One of the things that I love about OKRs is that they are quarterly. I tell people they can't change their goals during a quarter, but that you shouldn't spend time on it. You set your goals, and should stay focused on execution.

(*continued*)

Even if you have the wrong goals, it's better to learn from that than go through the process of resetting goals."

Hug said he loves the continuous improvement and flexible aspect of OKRs.

"We are always learning what are the better things for us to focus on and refine our focus. I like to embrace that but not really screw around with the goals mid-quarter."

16

Key Business Rhythm: Annual Planning

ANNUAL PLANNING TIMELINE OVERVIEW

ONE TO THREE MONTHS PRIOR TO THE NEW YEAR	ONE MONTH PRIOR TO THE NEW YEAR	FIRST FEW WEEKS OF THE NEW YEAR
Executives and senior leadership begin annual planning meetings and conversations.	Executives and senior leadership communicate company-level OKRs to team leaders.	Team leaders should roll out Q1 team OKRs, making sure to communicate the right expectations for the upcoming quarter to their team.
Executives and senior leadership draft and reconcile company-level annual OKRs, as well as Q1 company OKRs.	Team leaders and senior leadership discuss team priorities and focus for the upcoming year.	Team leaders should start scheduling regular check-ins, mid-quarter reviews, and end-of-quarter reviews with team members.
	Team leaders write team's Q1 OKRs that align with company-level OKRs.	

Annual planning is the most critical piece in setting your business up for success for the year. With a concrete plan, you'll gain a clear idea of where your organization is headed, how you'll define success, and a clear understanding of how you'll execute your organization's biggest priorities.

The power in OKRs is that they provide a roadmap to reach your most important and ambitious goals, and give you the waypoints to chart a course you may not have ever thought possible.

If unexpected roadblocks happen along the way, your business will have the ability to adjust and adapt much more efficiently if everyone knows the most important work needed to move the business forward.

Annual planning is a process. It's going to take time to map out, but it will be well worth it in preparing your teams for the year ahead. In this chapter, I walk you step-by-step through the key components of planning with OKRs. I include details about what you need to do at the leadership level, down to how every individual will be involved in the business's most important goals. At the end of this chapter, you should know exactly where your company is headed in the new year and how you are going to achieve your most ambitious plans.

Key Business Rhythm: One to Three Months Before the Start of Next Year

Who needs to be involved: Executives and senior-level leadership.

What needs to happen: For smaller companies with prior OKR experience, I recommend the leadership start annual planning four to six weeks before the start of the new year. For larger companies, or companies without OKR experience, I recommend that executives and senior-level leadership begin the process of discussing annual company goals for the new year two to three months prior to the start of the year. This will also be the time to discuss first-quarter company goals as well.

Reflection Before Creation

It's important to reflect on this past year's annual goals before you begin developing new goals for the new year. If all of the annual goals your organization implemented a year ago still apply perfectly today, you are in the minority. When it comes to OKRs, it's always a learning experience. Even if you hit 100% for an OKR, there's always something you can take away from it.

These discussions during the annual planning process may not just be one or two meetings, and it might take a few weeks to complete them, giving your team time to step away and digest, and then come back together for another session. Be realistic about how much time this will take and the key stakeholders that need to be involved in the decision making.

When reflecting on the past year's annual goals, make sure to ask these questions:

- Which goals are not applicable right now?
- How much did any major events (i.e., COVID, external market forces, war, global events) affect our completion of annual goals?
- Which goals do we want to roll over for the new year?
- What have we learned from the goals we didn't reach?
- Did we write good OKRs? If not, how do we improve upon that for the new year?
- Celebrate wins!

Assess Current Gaps and Problem Areas

A central part of annual planning is getting honest about the areas where you need more focus, or have external risks to be aware of. Focus holistically on the operational challenges you face.

1. **The market and industry:** Are we not moving quickly enough? Are we stable enough to withstand volatility?

2. **Cross-functionally:** Are we aligned between departments? Do we have overlap or dependencies that aren't being addressed today?

3. **Team ability:** Do we have the right people working on the right things? Are there liabilities in specific areas of the business that we should address through our planning?

4. **Resourcing:** Budgets, hiring plans, time allocation are all involved. Your job as a leadership team is to provide the guardrails for the rest of the company so they have an idea of what they can reasonably take on through their OKR planning process.

These gaps are likely areas you have addressed or are at the very least aware of, but a detailed accounting and plan to address will set the tone for this program.

Key Business Rhythm: One Month Prior to the New Year

Who needs to be involved: Senior leadership and department or team leaders.

What needs to happen: By December, senior leadership should communicate with directors and team leaders on annual company-level goals and how those will translate to each team's quarterly goals. Discussion with team leaders is key to ensuring that every team understands the priorities and focus for the upcoming year.

If team leaders need more training on OKRs, this is an ideal time to make sure they have the support and coaching they need on OKR best practices. Plan to run interactive workshops to help engage and educate teams during this time if they are not already familiar with the OKR framework. A refresher also never hurts.

Key Business Rhythm: The First Week of the New Year

Who needs to be involved: The entire company.

What needs to happen: In the first few weeks of the new year, the senior leadership team will share the business level OKRs with the company, and team leaders should roll out drafts of current cycle's team OKRs, making sure to communicate the right expectations for the upcoming period. Remember, the cycles can be flexible and should reflect the most appropriate rhythm for your business. This is the time to start scheduling regular check-ins and plan for reviews, as well as time for everyone to score and review OKRs at the end of the first quarter. The cycle repeats itself each quarter, with team and company-level quarterly OKRs always keeping alignment with the company's annual goals.

17

Key Business Rhythm: Quarterly OKR Planning

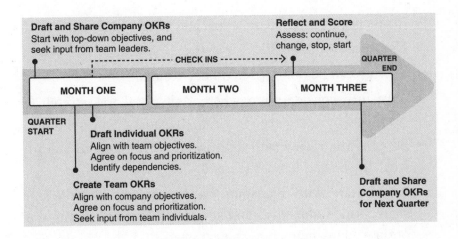

Draft and Share Company OKRs
Start with top-down objectives, and seek input from team leaders.

Reflect and Score
Assess: continue, change, stop, start

------------- CHECK INS ------------->

QUARTER END

| MONTH ONE | MONTH TWO | MONTH THREE |

QUARTER START

Draft Individual OKRs
Align with team objectives.
Agree on focus and prioritization.
Identify dependencies.

Create Team OKRs
Align with company objectives.
Agree on focus and prioritization.
Seek input from team individuals.

Draft and Share Company OKRs for Next Quarter

For the most part, OKRs are planned on an annual basis and a quarterly basis, with more emphasis on the quarterly process. This makes the quarterly review process critical.

End-of-Quarter OKR Scoring and Reflections

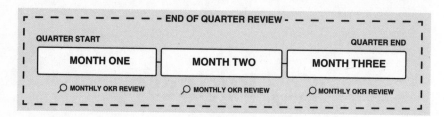

Who needs to be involved: The leader who owns an OKR and the team responsible for helping reach it.

What needs to happen: The end of quarter review is an opportunity for teams, managers, and individuals to review their progress and reflect on the performance of the previous quarter. These meetings are when OKRs are assessed and scored.

The goal of the quarterly review is to:

- Assess progress based on a goal and assign a score.
- Use a scale of 0.0–1.0.
- Scoring can be done based on key results.
- Take into consideration whether the goal was stretch or committed.
- Support the review and discussions with teams to identify wins, losses, and lessons learned.
- Collaborate with managers on quarter-end meetings to share graded objectives and key results, explain results, and outline adjustments for the next quarter.

"One of the things that is really important and key to a goal-setting framework is you have to stay focused on the future and not beat yourself up over the past," says Josh Hug, COO and co-founder of Remitly. "That's what we try to foster. We want to learn from the past and do better in the future."

Remember from Chapter 11 that you should enter in any final values for key results, as either a percentage (i.e., 80% complete) or a metric (i.e., $50,000 in sales), and use this scoring model (most OKR tools, like the one we built, does this automatically for you).

SCORE	COLOR
≤ 0.4	RED
0.5–0.6	ORANGE
0.7–0.9	GREEN
1.0	ORANGE

Closing out your quarterly or annual OKRs is an important time to stop and reflect on both performance and process:

OKR Performance

- What objectives did I complete successfully, and why?
- What issues did my team or I struggle with?
- Was I way too ambitious, and need to scale back and focus more?
- Or did I sell myself short and not set my goals high enough?

- What lessons were learned that can be applied to the next period?
- What do we want to start doing, stop doing, or continue doing in the next period?

OKR Process

- What OKRs can be rewritten to be more effective in the next quarter?
- What technology integrations can be added to streamline our process?
- What reports and dashboards can be created to easily track progress?
- What additional training is needed for leaders and employees?

Each time you close out your OKRs, the process should be smoother than the last, and the task of "close out old OKRs, set new ones" should become an ingrained part of your routine.

Assume you'll spend a week reflecting and closing out your annual goals, and a day or two closing out your goals each quarter.

The OKR scoring and review meetings are critical to this program's success. They require your team to prepare and thoughtfully distill the work that they've been doing on a monthly or quarterly basis.

Doing so in a group setting requires an accurate account and level of accountability that the team needs in order to take the process seriously and apply rigor to their own application.

One red flag to watch out for is your team feeling like OKRs are a method of monitoring. Remember that the score is less important than continually learning from the OKR process.

The last thing you want is for them to feel like this is more work on their plate that is solely designed to keep tabs on their productivity. Ensure that they are focused on their connection to the broader mission of the company, and that they are invested in the impact they can make, by keeping OKRs from being a punitive lever.

18

Key Business Rhythm: Monthly OKR Reviews

Who needs to be involved: Monthly OKR reviews may include stakeholders from senior leadership and/or other teams and departments, for transparency, but should be run by the owner of that OKR.

What needs to happen: The focus of these meetings should be on reviewing behind or at-risk OKRs, with an emphasis on blockers and the actions that can correct the course of the OKR. Schedule these meetings in advance and give employees proper notice to prepare.

Before the meeting, OKRs should be updated with commentary and with everyone prepared to discuss the at-risk or behind OKRs.

I know that the last thing many of us want is yet another meeting on our calendars, but remember that OKRs should be the connective tissue in everything your organization does— and to enact this vitally, they must be revisited on a regular basis. Consider making OKRs a focal point of already existing monthly meetings.

Other meetings that can be reframed around OKRs:

1. **Monthly "town hall" meetings**
   Consider holding a company-wide meeting once a month that goes further in depth on the state of the company than the weekly meetings. The "state" of the company should be driven by where OKR progress stands. This is also a great opportunity for employees to participate by asking questions and making suggestions. *You can fold this into an already existing meeting of this type.*

2. **Cross-functional OKR meetings and Agile sprints**
   In addition to the flow of information, as a leadership team, it shows a commitment to the company's objectives to plan scheduled cross-functional meetings with stakeholders who "own" a piece of each OKR. For example, if you have an objective around 10x revenue growth, you could hold a biweekly meeting with sales, customer service, marketing, and product stakeholders who have cascaded OKRs supporting that topic. *You can fold this into an already existing meeting of this type.*

19

Key Business Rhythm: Weekly Team Meetings

Who needs to be involved: The department's leader and their team.

What needs to happen: Framing regular team meetings around OKRs keeps goals top of mind. This way, the meeting doesn't get sidetracked, and the team can stay focused on the most important work that needs to get done. Having this meeting sets the tone for the week, and reminds everyone that OKRs should drive the work that they're doing, not the other way around. We all know what it's like when meetings get in the way of actual work being done, so if you're going to have a meeting with your team, make sure the discussion is meaningful.

What to discuss during your weekly OKR meetings (which can become a part of already scheduled meetings):

Overall Progress

❑ Discuss check-ins that have been made over the past week.
❑ If many objectives have had "nothing new to report" check-ins, this will help identify what's moving forward and what's not.

At-Risk/Behind Objectives

❑ Identify each of these objectives and, with their owner, have an open conversation to understand why they are behind or at risk, what their owner's plan is for the coming week, and if any revisions need to be made.
❑ Ideas and feedback from all team members is helpful in this section to formulate plans for getting back on track.

Focus for the Upcoming Week

❑ For each objective that is incomplete, identify what actions will be taken by its owner in the upcoming week to continue progress for the quarter.

Action Items

❑ Document any other tasks that need to be completed prior to next week's meeting.

These meetings are about alignment and transparency. Keep those core values top of mind in order to foster the right context for the team.

Other Weekly Meetings

1. **Weekly internal leadership meetings**

   Rethink your weekly meeting with the department heads to discuss progress across teams. Connecting every department reinforces that OKRs should be top of mind and drive the work being done to help the company reach its goals. Including all team leaders helps eliminate silos and ultimately, if there are issues, they can be addressed more efficiently. At the end of the quarter, use this meeting as an opportunity to go over what went wrong, what went right, and what the plan is for the future quarter.

2. **Weekly organization-wide meetings**

   Company leaders should also consider holding a regular company-wide meeting at the beginning of the week where leadership can discuss important updates or issues the company is having and give all employees the opportunity to ask questions. This can be a quick 30-minute meeting that is structured by going over progress of the company's goals for the quarter or another given time period.

3. **Key initiative meetings**

   For each key initiative outlined in your OKRs, you should already have a mechanism in place to gather stakeholders who are involved in that initiative. This has been deemed a core priority. Get the functional team together once a week to share status updates, discuss potential roadblocks and challenges, and make decisions around predetermined special topics. My recommendation is request agenda items a few days before the meeting, and also create space for each stakeholder to give updates on their line tems.

20

Key Business Rhythm: 1:1 Meetings

Who needs to be involved: A manager and their direct report.

What needs to happen: In a world where "virtual meeting fatigue" is a very real thing, squeezing in yet another meeting to your already jam-packed schedule might not seem very appealing, which is why structuring 1:1s effectively is so important.

As a leader in your organization, your direct reports are counting on you to give them the feedback they crave to be productive at work. What's more, it's in your best interest to hear from the front lines of your business so that you can make informed decisions. Enter the 1:1 meeting, designed around your OKRs to create continuous feedback loops.

Before the Meeting

Select the frequency of your meetings:

❏ Weekly 1:1s are the most common, especially between managers and direct reports. Scale back to biweekly if that feels like too much, using Slack or email for a quick offline check-in during the off week.

❏ Monthly or quarterly 1:1s are best for touching base with other key employees in your organization, or for companies where a manager has a very large number of direct reports.

Choose a day and time: Most managers choose early in the week for 1:1s, in order to set action items that need to get done that week, or late in the week to review progress and prepare for the following week. Much like getting a workout in before you start your day, choosing a time earlier in the morning makes it less likely that your day gets away from you or that putting out a fire causes you to cancel your 1:1.

It doesn't matter so much what day or time you choose, but that you're consistent. Continually postponing or arriving late to a 1:1 can be extremely frustrating for an employee, sending a message that their time isn't valuable, so honor your calendar.

Update OKRs: Have team members do an OKR check-in before the meeting so their progress is up to date. Framing team meetings around OKRs keeps goals top of mind, prevents getting sidetracked, and helps focus on the most important work to be done. Keep in mind, not every 1:1 should be about OKRs. There are many other focuses and topics that are important, but as part of the cadence, a regular 1:1 focused on OKRs is important. I recommend doing this at least once per month.

Set the agenda: The most effective 1:1s start with a clear agenda. Make sure OKRs are a part of that agenda at least once per month, and that the participants are prepared to discuss. An OKR software platform will generally offer notification reminders that can be customized to send a nudge to check in on the day and time you prefer.

- ❑ **Informal check-in:** Resist the urge to dive immediately into business goals to kick off your meeting. Instead, take five minutes to chat about life outside of work, from pets and kids to the latest binge-worthy series. Swapping personal stories about your weekend or passion projects for just a few minutes each week builds trust and communication over time, especially in a remote-only world. Note: Additionally, it's often prudent to ask if there are any urgent items that need to be addressed right off the bat. If an employee has an irate customer, a family issue they are dealing with, or is preoccupied with their commission check, it might be hard for them to concentrate before that item is addressed.

- ❑ **Review team and individual OKRs:** What is going well? Start with some wins! Ask the employee to highlight OKRs that made significant progress over the past week and what they learned from them. Where are there blockers? As a manager, you should be asking, "How can I help?" "Where are people getting stuck?" and "How can I help remove obstacles to success?" If the scope of the objective needs to change, have that conversation here. For example, does an at-risk objective need additional resources to be allocated, or should it be reprioritized or revised based on new information?

- ❑ **Action items:** For each objective that is incomplete, identify what actions will be taken in the upcoming week to continue progress for the quarter. It's important to get specific. Instead of "Finish up the training download" get details like

"Rachel to complete content by EOD Monday, get Katrina's design signoff by Thursday, and upload the final version to the LMS on Friday."

❑ **Wrapping up:** As the meeting winds down, cover any items that didn't make the agenda or weren't on OKRs, such as upcoming time off or personal development goals like additional training. Take this opportunity to jot down some notes about the session.

FAQs for OKR Check-Ins

What content should be included in an OKR check-in? Your OKR check-in should contain the data update for each key result and key initiative, alongside a short commentary to add any qualitative context to the data. An example of this update would be "Our product was mentioned in close to 50% of the total press articles about our industry because of our company event. We doubled our goal of 110 articles, and this becomes our new baseline for large-moment press adoption."

How should you run an OKR check-in meeting?

An OKR check-in meeting should have the expectation set that all check-ins are made *prior* to the meeting itself.

From there, the meeting conversation should primarily focus on those OKRs that are behind or at-risk; a dashboard with an OKR list widget that filters for just those statuses can be helpful to facilitate this conversation.

The conversation on the behind or at-risk OKRs should primarily revolve around a collaborative discussion on how to get those OKRs back on track, and each conversation should conclude with a clear set of next steps and ownership.

Timeboxing the conversation to a predefined amount of time (based on the volume of OKRs on the agenda and meeting duration) can be helpful to ensure that all relevant OKRs are covered.

At the end of the meeting, if time permits, the team can review the other OKRs.

How do you check in on dependencies across an OKR?

Reviewing dependencies should happen asynchronously by the owner of the objective or key result that has identified those dependencies. That individual should monitor the status of the dependent OKRs by adding those objects to their own dashboard in the platform.

On an as-needed basis, meetings or messaging to connect with the owners of the dependencies should happen in order to ensure continued alignment. This can be done through existing communication channels, or by tagging a user in their check-in commentary.

How do I know when it's time to change goals?

By the time the first day of the quarter (or work cycle) has arrived, your company's goals should already be set. Why? I always emphasize starting the planning process early in the previous period so that your team is prepared to hit the ground running.

When you plan in advance, your team can know exactly what is expected of them for the cycle ahead and where they need to focus their efforts.

In an ideal world, your team will be able to follow these targets the entire period, moving toward reaching their goals and achieving them without any adjustments. That's how it should work every time—you plan, and then the plans get achieved. Unfortunately, this isn't always the case.

Changes come up for any number of reasons—new needs and projects arise, supply chain disruptions occur, and suddenly you realize that your team's goals may need to shift.

When should we make mid-cycle changes to our goals and targets and when should we stick with it and learn or change?

You should make mid-cycle changes to your goals when:

1. A more important priority arises and the current goal will no longer receive the attention or bandwidth required to make meaningful progress.

2. It becomes clear that the goal was not desirable, economically viable, or feasible.

3. When you uncover an insight that suggests the goal should be adjusted.

Examples

You set a goal to launch a new sales enablement tool by a certain date, but realize that things outside of your control are preventing you from moving forward. Or, you realized that you were focused on a less opportune segment of the market.

In this case, you might adjust the goal to start a new project, stop the existing one, or continue with some sort of adjustment to project scope.

Another real-life example is when a client recently set a goal around launching a new innovation project in a specific segment, but then decided to acquire another company in said segment a few weeks into the quarter. In this case, the OKR was postponed.

What should we do with unforeseen disruptions?

Unforeseen and unexpected events should lead to a discussion between the objective owner and key members of their management chain to confirm prioritization in lieu of this event. For example, a supply chain disruption could mean that you won't be able to hit your fulfillment targets as expected. In this case you have two options:

1. You could adjust your fulfillment forecasts and cascade these changes to all OKRs that are impacted by it.
2. You could hold the goals steady, but then spend time thinking about how to fill the gap/achieve the goal in spite of the limitation (many great innovations have been discovered amid limitations).

Consider reprioritizing your objectives, which might potentially lead to the closing or postponement of a goal.

What happens when teams are starting to fall short on their OKRs?

You have a few options when teams start falling short on OKRs.

Depending on the nature of the goals (whether they are aspirational or committed), you could remind your team that pursuing goals is about learning so that you can be even better next time. This is especially true for aspirational goals. Doubling down on intellectual safety and giving people permission to fail can be a really great way to empower creativity in your ranks.

For committed goals in particular, you can still focus on learning and discovery, but with an even greater focus on making immediate adjustments to rapidly change the goal's trajectory.

From there you can start to identify "quick wins" that could help bring initiatives back on track. You might also discover other more fundamental challenges that need to be resolved over time (for example, lack of access to clean and reliable data, the need to hire more people, etc.).

Above all else, when your team is demoralized, remind them of what they have accomplished and what is going well. One of my favorite things to say is: "Okay, you got to 40%. Let's talk about filling that gap to 100% in a moment, but first: What did you do to even get to 40% in the first place?"

What are best practices for executing changes and communicating to the appropriate stakeholders?

Keep communications focused on learning over judgment. When you make a change, make sure you have a clearly articulated, succinct rationale for the adjustment. Why did we make the change? What value are we trying to achieve with this new approach? What will we *not* do?

Changes mid-cycle can feel like progress toward goals is being jeopardized. This is not necessarily true. The ability to make adjustments mid-quarter is precisely why we recommend doing check-ins on a regular basis—it is far better for you to make a change in the middle of the quarter than to continue down a path set up to fail until the beginning of the next cycle.

Instead of viewing a change as a failure, view it as an opportunity to stay focused on outcomes and not just outputs.

OKRs in the Real World

Creating a Common Language with WORKSOFT

Creating a high-performance culture is a top priority for many companies in competitive, fast-changing markets. WORKSOFT is no exception.

WORKSOFT provides enterprise organizations with a continuous test automation platform for their applications, which is designed to help QA teams "reliably deliver flawless applications faster and more efficiently." One could argue that the business was built for these fast-moving, ever-changing environments.

But growing silos within the organization inspired new CEO Tony Sumpster to prioritize the company's culture, and drive tighter alignment across different functions and teams. Although many employees were highly engaged and passionate about their work, there was a greater need for fluid collaboration that inspired transparency and open communication—especially around big-picture ideas and strategic initiatives.

Sumpster brought in Kathy Eastwood, a leadership coach and HR executive, to help WORKSOFT implement the principles and practices that tackle these internal challenges and help build a collaborative, high-performance organization. They embarked on a three-stage process that included goal-setting, tactical planning, and employee engagement and alignment. Implementing OKRs played a crucial role in every step of the process.

The first stage required Kathy to align with the executive team and map their goals to a more comprehensive three-year plan developed by Tony Sumpster. The multiyear strategy was then redesigned as annual OKRs and executive leadership began tracking progress in weekly team meetings. "We made the decision in the first quarter to manage OKRs with just the executives," Kathy said. "The CFO and I ran every single meeting on OKRs, with the dashboard out and walking through every task, how we would accomplish our goals, and what was needed to ensure success." This got the whole team rallying around a common set of goals, which helped the entire executive team communicate and collaborate better.

"One thing our CEO has said is 'we have to stop talking and we have to start doing.' OKRs allow us to look at the big picture and consider what tasks are realistic in the bigger picture."

Once OKRs were fully embedded into executive conversations, the next step was to get all employees on board. To get all employees bought in to the vision, WORKSOFT gave them all access to view goals across the company, and broke annual goals into quarterly goals and team-based goals. After introducing the framework, the software used to manage it, and hosting a one-hour training session, WORKSOFT saw 99% participation within a week.

While some teams gravitated quickly to OKRs and were "religious" about using the methodology, others had to go through an iterative process to understand how these OKRs could drive their everyday tasks and help them focus on the work that matters. It also has been an ongoing journey to build employee trust and transparency in the organization around using OKRs, especially since some were fearful of repercussions if they didn't accomplish their specific goals. The executive team has focused on alleviating these concerns by openly communicating the importance of setting big goals, encouraging more risk

(*continued*)

taking, and supporting failure if it leads to personal and professional growth.

OKRs have cultivated a more rallying spirit within WORKSOFT by improving cross-team visibility and collaboration. Powerful integrations allow users to connect OKR software with Jira, Smartsheet, and Salesforce, which has helped streamline workflows and create a comprehensive view of tasks and progress towards larger goals. Team managers also use OKRs for performance conversations on a daily basis to track employee progress and add notes about their unique goals, accomplishments, and challenges. This helps improve team transparency and allows managers to have more productive conversations that use a consistent, more objective language.

"OKRs really help teams define what success looks like and what the outcome is," Kathy says. "This allows managers to set goals and expectations up front and have more productive conversations with employees if they're not following through on those expectations."

All team-level OKRs ladder up to larger, companywide goals in order to show employees how their daily work impacts the business's strategic direction and overall growth. And by documenting and managing OKRs in a central location, all members of the organization—from the executive team to employees—can easily track progress and prioritize tasks.

Overall, WORKSOFT has seen upticks in productivity and plans to run a series of qualitative and quantitative surveys to assess this performance against employee sentiment and satisfaction rates. Although the organization is still working to quantify the big-picture value for the business, Kathy says she has already seen a massive improvement in employee trust and passion: "For now, it's all a feeling."

Defining purpose, drafting objectives, and establishing measurements can have a "finished" state. The process through which you create organizational change does not. It's ongoing, and takes commitment from both the champion and sponsor, but also the rest of the organization.

This commitment takes on a very real form: meetings, documentation, and reviews can be easy to give up on. By committing to the process, and enabling broad adoption and implementation, an OKR program can soar, driving real results for the business. In the next section of this book, you'll learn how to bring these business rhythms to life with the best practices for implementing and rolling out an OKR program effectively.

IV

Getting Started with OKRs

Implementing and benefiting from OKRs in your organization is not a "set it and forget it," one-time process. It requires a phased approach to build a program at the heart of your business and organizational culture. You will continue to iterate and grow over time.

I talk about this phased approach in terms of your organization's "OKR maturity" which is represented visually on the following page.

BEGINNING	PILOTING	ADOPTING	SCALING	CENTERING
				Unlocking cultural buy-in for OKRs
			Rolling out OKRs broadly	✓ Executive sponsorship
		Committing to the OKR practice	✓ Executive sponsorship	✓ Team members reference OKRs in every decision, big and small
	Validating OKRs in your organization		✓ OKRs are rolled out to the rest of the company and baked into large, organization-wide initiatives	✓ OKRs are firmly entrenched in business rhythms, becoming a global mindset of focus and alignment
Starting your OKR journey	✓ Organizational experimentation with OKR methodology via pilot group	✓ Executive sponsorship ✓ Top levels of the organization are developing the OKR muscle and habit	✓ OKRs are firmly embedded in business rhythms throughout the organization, from top to bottom	✓ Employees feel there is purpose at the center of everything they do
✓ No usage of OKR methodology	✓ Small group learning OKR concept and building into business rhythm	✓ OKRs are expanding more widely into business rhythms	✓ OKR tool is selected and used across the organization	
✓ No structured business rhythm	✓ Small group trying to understand how OKRs will work for them at scale	✓ OKR tool selection begins		
✓ Limited alignment of goals between levels				
1	2	3	4	5

Any strong OKR program that empowers a team to move the needle for the business has several characteristics in common:

- **Organization-wide adoption of OKRs**

    When only a part of the team is aware of and using OKRs, you cannot reap the benefits of organization-wide alignment and transparency that makes the OKR framework so powerful. The entire organization should be aware of OKRs, how the company is using them, and how they can participate.

- **OKRs underpin culture of the organization**

    OKRs should never be an afterthought, and instead should be a part of daily life at your organization. OKR terminology and concepts should be a normal part of conversation, and employees should use OKRs as a guide for what to prioritize.

- **Executive sponsorship**

    One of the most important parts of organization-wide OKR adoption is getting senior executives on board.

Executives should model the proper use of OKRs and encourage employees to do the same. What does this mean in practice? Executives must share OKRs regularly as central to how they think about and run the business, from presentations at company-wide meetings to how they frame up questions for department leads.

- **Established business rhythms**

   OKRs are only valuable if you use them to drive the decisions made and work being done. This happens through a strong cadence of meetings and communication. Rhythms can incorporate daily, weekly, monthly, and quarterly touches that inform and drive employee execution. A fully mature OKR system will have key meetings defined for the entire year, and team-level meetings scheduled for the current quarter.

   Note that you do not need to add an entirely new set of rhythms to your organization to accommodate OKRs. Instead, existing rhythms can be modified to incorporate OKRs, such as weekly status meetings, standups, or email updates beginning with the latest OKR status.

- **Greater transparency across levels and teams**

   OKRs should be transparent and accessible to the entire organization, to the extent this is possible for your organization. Some sensitive OKRs, such as finances of a public company, must have limited visibility only to senior staff, but the vast majority of OKRs should be visible to all.

   This is part of why we roll out OKRs—because we know that when my team understands what your team is working on, why, and how our efforts relate to one another, everyone is more engaged and aligned, making it easier to understand and achieve business goals.

- **Greater alignment across teams and organization**

  Goals should be aligned to overarching objectives so that employees can trace their work to the organization-wide level. By understanding the strategic direction of the executive leadership team, employees are better equipped to understand how their own goals should be written to align with organization-wide aspirations.

- **Enhanced learning and reflection**

  Scoring should be completed in parallel with deep reflection exercises that evaluate both team and OKR performance at the end-of-cycle review. Reflecting on progress is important when evaluating what could be done differently or better during the following quarter.

- **Dedicated ownership of OKR program and change management**

  Your OKR program should be managed by employees who have time allocated for communications, process refinement, stakeholder engagement, and continuous improvement initiatives. Critically, this team should have its own OKRs for how effectively it is delivering value to the organization via the OKR program. Like Agile scrum masters, this dedicated focus becomes less critical as OKRs become part of the organization's fabric.

These elements, when properly implemented, will come together to bring your organization to full OKR maturity—your ideal state.

In this section, I provide the building blocks getting started on your path toward OKR maturity in your organization, beginning with laying out the key roles—OKR champion, executive, manager, and individual—and ending with a step-by-step process for bringing OKRs into the fold.

22

Key Roles in Getting Started with OKRs

For OKRs to drive growth throughout the organization, there are several key players who need to be invested in their success. Here, I outline the broader set of stakeholders, and then dig in on five specific roles: The executive sponsor, the OKR champions, the team managers, the individual contributor, and the HR leader.

First up is the **executive sponsor**, who is integral to a successful OKR program. This is the leader who understands that OKRs can be a wind of (positive) change in their organization, works to make sure other leaders see this vision, and communicates regularly with the OKR champion to make sure the leadership team is providing the guidance and reinforcement necessary to embed OKRs in the DNA of the organization.

The **CEO or department leader**, whether they are the sponsor or not, will drive buy-in on the value of OKRs and set the tone by drafting organization-wide OKRs and ensuring clear and actionable priorities are defined, at the business level.

The **strategy and operations leader** (often a COO or CSO) is responsible for change management and operational efficiency, including strategic alignment, across the organization.

The **human resources executive** (often a CHRO within enterprise companies) is responsible for buy-in on the value for employee engagement, and is able to articulate the relationship to performance management and compensation.

The next fundamental role is the **OKR champion**, who is the point of contact and driving force of the OKR program. In an enterprise, there will be several champions who form a cross-departmental team. Got a question about OKRs? This is your go-to person.

The **IT leader** (often a chief information officer within enterprise companies) is a critical partner in managing the deployment and availability of an OKR solution.

The **team manager** is an equally important force for change within the organization, ensuring that teams are trained up and engaged with OKRs and the OKR writing, management, and scoring process.

Finally we have the **individual contributor**, your end user, the person who you need to make sure adopts and uses OKRs regularly. If individual contributors in your organization do not experience the value of OKRs for themselves, you've got a bottleneck you have to resolve, using the resources of OKR champion, executive sponsor, and team manager. The good news is, with software tools available that give you line-of-sight into usage and progress, you won't have to take a shot in the dark to understand how your organization is faring with OKRs from the ground up, so you can make the necessary changes to move forward.

Let's start by delving deeper into the key role of the executive sponsor.

Executive Sponsor

EXECUTIVE SPONSOR

✓ Buys in to value OKRs

✓ OKR Beginning[+]

✓ Gets the organization onboard

✓ Heavy organizational influence across and down

The Executive Sponsor's Role in OKRs

As a leader within the organization, the executive sponsor's role is to provide sponsorship so that OKRs can be integrated into the DNA of the organization.

Top level buy-in for the OKR process is key. Founders and CEOs need to make the successful implementation of OKRs a priority and message this throughout the organization on a regular basis. In larger organizations, large groups or divisions can act as "seed" organizations for implementing OKRs.

THE EXECUTIVE SPONSOR

Executive sponsors are members of the executive leadership team that provide strong backing and support for the overall OKR program.

WHAT THEY DO:	WHAT IT TAKES:
✓ Showcase the value of OKRs to the broader employee base	✓ Two hours per week, on average
✓ Integrate OKRs into the way they lead across the company	✓ OKR education: this book, *Measure What Matters*, and *Redical Focus*
✓ Provide vocal sponsorship for an OKR program	✓ Regular conversations with the OKR champion to understand and address feedback
✓ Ensure that appropriate investments are made for the OKR program	

RECOMMENDATION: MINIMUM OF ONE EXECUTIVE SPONSOR.

There are four keys to being successful as an executive sponsor:

1. **Communicate the importance of OKRs.**

   It's up to the executive sponsor to communicate the importance of OKRs to their organization, helping everyone understand why OKRs are essential to success and how they connect to the current culture. This includes activities like:
   - Kicking off the conversation about OKRs leadership- and company-wide, and expressing enthusiasm about them.
   - Making sure that every employee is crystal clear on why OKRs are being brought on board and how they will benefit.
   - Reinforcing OKRs and their central placement in the organization by making OKRs a part of every communication, including written communication and presentations.

2. **Work with the executive team to draft OKRs.**

   First, craft your company's top three to five objectives for the year. As an executive sponsor, it's important to start with the end in mind so that focus on the mission and vision becomes intrinsically connected to the OKR process throughout the company. What does success look like for your company this year? What needs to be the primary focus for each division, department, or team in order to make that success a reality? How is every department-level goal connected to the broader mission and strategy?

   With that clarity, it's an executive sponsor's responsibility, with the executive team, to craft the company's top three to five objectives for the year.

   Next, it's time to define quarterly company objectives. Once the executive sponsor and executive team have decided on the company's top three to five objectives for the year, it's time to define the quarterly company objectives.

These objectives should be aligned with the annual objectives and give teams across the organization guidance as to which work they should be prioritizing.

3. **Participate actively in using OKRs to align the business.**

   The executive sponsor is responsible for activities that make OKRs a part of the business rhythm, like:
   - Sharing OKRs publicly and regularly with the organization, including sharing progress toward OKRs at town halls and company-wide meetings.
   - Involving OKRs as a central component of leadership team meetings and presentation decks.
   - Supporting regular employee training for OKRs.
   - Asking for and reviewing feedback on the OKR process often, then addressing that feedback head-on.

   This investment today creates major progress for not only the health of your OKR program but the health of your business as you move forward and up the OKR maturity model path.

4. **Be patient and provide support.**

   If your team is new to OKRs, they will go through the inevitable ups and downs of any change during the OKR adoption period. The best thing you can do to be successful with OKRs is acting as a cheerleader for the team and helping them cross the chasm. The change will likely take a few cycles, but OKRs will provide significant long-term benefits.

   As the executive sponsor, you are the sounding board for questions and roadblocks that your executive team and even larger team (via your OKR champion) are experiencing.

This means:

- Enabling people to focus on fewer things, including avoiding the temptation to ask team members to take on work that is not related to company-wide OKRs.

- Setting up regular time to sync with OKR champions on the feedback from the larger team and take action based on what you hear.

- Setting up and reinforcing a "growth mindset" culture, not maintaining the status quo—along with making it clear that reaching 70% of your OKRs is great if the goals were ambitious enough.

Being the executive sponsor also requires asking the tough questions that open up the right conversations to move the business forward.

The executive sponsor should use OKRs as they're intended: to make sure everyone is focused on the work that matters, from other executives to team leaders to individual contributors. Part of this process is asking tough questions and opening up conversations that may have felt too "hot to touch" before. These questions include:

- **"Which OKR does this align to?"** when talking about bringing new projects or initiatives on board—or even discussions about resourcing and hiring

- **"What will we deprioritize to accommodate this new OKR?"** to make it clear to other leaders that the company has a commitment to relentless focus, enabled by the OKR framework

- **"Why aren't we making more progress on this OKR?"** to provide a safe space for obtaining clarity and ensuring accountability across leadership and the broader organization

OKR Champion

OKR CHAMPION

✓ Passionate about goal-setting and driving organization change

✓ OKR Piloting[+]

✓ Implements and writes OKRs

✓ Champions OKRs to their teams

The OKR Champion's Role in OKRs

The OKR champion facilitates the OKR process and drives adoption, either across the entire organization or within their department as part of a broader cross-functional OKR champion group, including many important tasks. In large organizations, having a dedicated subculture of OKR champions who have gone above and beyond the typical end-user training ensures appropriate organic expansion and excitement. In smaller organizations, this can be a single person who drives the entire process. Either way, this is the most critical role in the OKR process. Without a champion moving people forward and maintaining the right cadence and process, any transformative process is bound to fail.

THE OKR CHAMPION

OKR champions play a key role in the rollout, adoption, and continuity of leveraging OKRs within an organization in a sustainable fashion, They are the connection points between different teams that help keep OKR programs on track.

WHAT THEY DO:

✓ Help other leaders communicate the vision behind change

✓ Coach fellow colleagues on OKR methodology and software

✓ Facilitate OKR sessions, mainly creation and reflection

✓ Ensure OKRs are clear and aligned

✓ Direct people to helpful resources

✓ Improve how your teams practice OKRs

WHAT IT TAKES:

✓ About two to three hours per week on average

✓ High-potential employees who are curious, effective listeners, prone to solving problems and building quality relationships

✓ Senior leaderships support of champions

✓ Complete software training

RECOMMENDATION: 1 CHAMPION FOR EVERY 15 TO 50 EMPLOYEES.

There are four keys to success as an OKR champion:

1. Be the communications center for all things OKR-related.

OKR champions promote transparency and progress at all levels by communicating the value of everyone understanding each other's focus and work, regardless of level or role.

OKR champions set the stage for open communication and continuous feedback across teams, with managers, and the leadership team. They're also on the hook for helping remove roadblocks and other unforeseen challenges the team may run into.

2. Set organizational expectations for OKRs.

Another key responsibility of the OKR champion is to set expectations for the entire OKR program, including planning, check-ins, review cycles, cadence, and timelines. OKR champions are responsible for shepherding the organization through the following process:

Plan: Beginning of every quarter

✓ Department OKRs are defined based on the company OKRs

✓ Team and individual OKRs are created and aligned

Execute: Throughout the quarter

✓ Evaluate your OKR progress and discuss evaluation with senior management

✓ Address at-risk or off-track OKRs and course-correct where possible

Reflect: End the quarter

✓ Review performance with senior management, discuss achievements and lessons learned

✓ Define new quarterly OKRs

This needs to be clear to leaders and individuals alike so it becomes a part of the common workflow and understanding. This is not as simple as sending an email at the beginning of the quarter. It's an ongoing flywheel of reinforcing the importance of weekly, monthly, and quarterly meetings.

This includes regular meetings with the executive sponsor to share feedback and recommend any tweaks or new communications necessary based on how the OKR rollout is going.

3. **Set up training opportunities and hold teams accountable.**

The OKR champion is also responsible for encouraging focus and holding the team (at every level) accountable for the role they play. The champion should continue to stress the importance of OKR alignment and execution of the related work. They also should proactively train the team to understand the connection between the work each member of the team is doing and the broader OKRs. Remember, OKRs are an integral strategic function, not an incremental task for the sake of adding more work.

4. **Celebrate OKR wins.**

OKR champions shouldn't skimp on celebrations. Celebrate progress and innovation born out of the OKR process. By encouraging momentum and innovation, the team will become more invested in the process, and more invested in building even more momentum. Be sure to document these celebrations so you can refer back when appropriate.

"An OKR champion is a superuser that understands the ins and outs of OKRs and can support their optimal adoption within a company. OKR champions help

with the successful rollout, adoption, and use of OKRs within a company. Usually there are a number of OKR champions within a company depending on size. They typically come from different areas of the operating organization to better contextualize OKRs for their areas of responsibility."

—Joe Ottinger, OKR Advisors

Team Manager

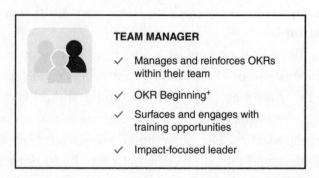

TEAM MANAGER

✓ Manages and reinforces OKRs within their team

✓ OKR Beginning[+]

✓ Surfaces and engages with training opportunities

✓ Impact-focused leader

The team manager enables team members to clearly understand the OKRs they need to drive, and the work they need to do to make the biggest impact. The team leader plays an important role in the success of the OKR framework and purpose.

By managing the OKR process within their team, a team manager takes on the role of teacher, advocate, and ambassador by managing the team by results and enabling them to achieve their goals, eliminating roadblocks so they can stay focused and achieve their goals, and proactively managing risks.

THE TEAM MANAGER

The team manager is the leader of a specific team in the organization who represents their working group of employees and function.

WHAT THEY DO:	WHAT IT TAKES:
✓ Serve as the voice of their organization to leadership	✓ About two to three hours per week, on average
✓ Own or co-own most objectives for their organization	✓ Building OKRs into team-wide and 1:1 coaching
✓ Model example OKR behavior for their team	✓ Guidance toward resources for team
✓ Enable their direct reports with opportunities to uplevel themselves on OKRs	✓ Participation as critical piece of the OKR feedback loop

There are four keys to being successful as a team manager:

1. **Schedule and participate in OKR team trainings.**

   OKRs are most likely a change to how your team has been doing things, shifting focus from activity/output to outcomes/impact. Some amount of training for your team will be required to accelerate the adoption of OKRs. Work with the OKR champion and facilitate training for your team.

   Show your team how engaged you are, ask questions in trainings, and follow up with your team members in meetings to see if they have any outstanding questions about OKRs, from writing them to using whatever tool you have brought on board to facilitate the process.

2. **Craft team OKRs that align to business OKRs.**

   The team manager should take team input to involve everyone in the process, then thoughtfully craft team OKRs that will motivate and inspire their team toward and beyond ambitious goals.

3. **Work with team members to build their individual OKRs when ready.**

   Once team OKRs have been shared with the team, the team manager should facilitate the process as team members build their own individual OKRs, making deadlines clear and checking in often to see what kind of support team members need, especially if the organization is a little earlier on in the maturity model.

   Individual OKRs should be added to your OKR program only after the team has become familiar with doing team-wide OKRs.

4. **Build and maintain team rituals that align to OKRs.**

   After team OKRs have been finalized at the company-wide, team, and individual levels, the team manager is responsible for normalizing OKRs as a part of daily work conversations and rituals. These include:

   - **1:1s:** "Can we pull up your OKRs and see how progress is going?"
   - **Dedicated OKR check-ins:** "Team, next week I'll be scheduling OKR check-ins with you [individually *or* as a group] to check in on progress and see how I can support you."
   - **Scoring and closing:** "Team, remember to close your OKRs and that we'll be reviewing where we netted out this quarter re: our goals in our next team meeting."
   - **Referencing OKRs at team meetings regularly:** "Let's go around the room and get a quick update on where everyone is at with their OKRs" or "Let's decide whether that should be a focus based on our OKRs for the quarter. I'll pull those up."

Individual Employees

In this section, I outline the role of individual contributor, but I spend more time focused on how to make the program valuable *for* these employees. In the end, their buy-in and investment will be critical to building a productive growth mindset using OKRs.

The individual plays a critical role in the OKR process. Each individual contributor is responsible for executing tactics that benefit the company mission. This is critical work, and the measures and outcomes of this work have to be documented regularly and thoroughly for the OKR process to be effective—hence why this book is titled *OKRs for All*, not *OKRs for Leadership* or *OKRs for Some*.

Making sure that every member of a team understands, can "speak," and is engaged with OKRs is the best way to make an OKR program successful. Without each employee owning OKRs, you don't just have employees who don't feel connected to company mission; the work they're doing doesn't connect to the mission, either, and that is a costly gamble.

Initially in an OKR rollout, individuals won't have individual OKRs, but every individual should be an observer, having visibility and maybe even a contributing role in coming up with company-wide OKRs, then department-wide and team-wide OKRs. While individuals don't have their own individual OKRs at this point, this transparency and ability to connect their everyday work to the higher-level OKRs is vital.

It also gets individual employees into the motion and rhythm of OKRs so that when individual OKR rollout happens, familiarity and participation are more likely.

There are four keys to being successful with OKRs as an individual contributor on a team:

1. **Learn about OKRs.**

   Leaders should provide individual contributors with the training and post-training resources they need to be successful, including check-ins on how OKRs are going.

   Individual contributors should leverage these resources to get up to speed with OKRs, ask for specified time to spend learning about OKRs if that hasn't been carved out organizationally, and ask for any other support needed that is not being given.

2. **Remember there are no stupid questions.**

   The best thing an organization can hope for is an engaged employee base that understands where the organization is headed and how they are contributing to that success.

   If you are an individual contributor, be proactive about raising your hand and asking questions about OKRs. OKRs are a valuable framework and mindset shift, but they can seem complex at first and take adjustment, like any new system or learning path. Chances are, if you have a question about OKRs, so does the person "next to you."

3. **Check in with your OKRs often.**

   A common mistake I've seen is team members spending time and energy writing their OKRs at the beginning of a time period, only to lose track of them as time passes by and distractions enter the picture. This defeats the purpose of OKRs, which is to bring teams closer to their purpose by a greater sense of focus.

   Set calendar reminders or use automation tools within your current OKR tool to ensure you're checking in with your OKRs on a regular basis—not just when the quarter is almost over or your boss asks you how OKRs are going. Usually, by that time, it's too late to make the adjustments necessary to stay on course.

4. **Give feedback.**

Hand-in-hand with asking questions, remember: feedback is a gift. If you're finding OKR adoption challenging or are unclear on the expectations of you, deliver this feedback to your manager so that you and your organization can continue to escalate up the OKR maturity curve.

The Human Resources Leader

The HR leader is integral to the success of any organization. As an HR leader, it's your job to manage succession planning, talent management, change management, performance management, training and development, and so much more. That's a big responsibility, especially given the immense challenges facing organizations and their employees today.

There are several reasons that the HR leader needs to be onboard with the OKR process:

1. HR is one of the few functional units in an organization that has access to the entire company. If we want OKR buy-in, we want to make sure that HR can help support the initiative.

2. HR often has dedicated budget and resources for training. Implementing OKR is like stretching a new muscle. If you need to train the whole organization, HR—or, more specifically, learning and development teams—can be a huge asset.

3. From an employee perspective, the first question you'll get is "How do OKRs affect my review, compensation, etc.?" You need HR on board to co-lead messaging about the relationship and differentiation between OKRs and performance management, and not provide different perspectives that can undermine the rollout.

4. Managers need support for OKRs. Not only do they have to apply OKRs to their jobs, but the spotlight falls on them when it comes to updates of OKRs. HR should make sure that managers are supported via coaching and training to know how to become strategic and how to be a proactive coach.

HR leaders are preparing their organizations for an employee exodus as 48% of American workers actively search for new jobs. The phenomenon is so prevalent across the workforce that it is being called the "Great Resignation."

One of the main drivers of this retention problem is a lack of engagement. With only 36% of employees reporting that they feel engaged in their work, it's no wonder that so many are considering leaving their roles for something more satisfying.

It also makes sense why, according to a PwC survey, these were the most critical areas of work for human resources leaders in 2021:

1. 90% of HR leaders said it's challenging to align business and HR priorities.

2. 66% said getting quality and credible employee data was a moderate or major challenge.

3. 37% said retaining employees was one of their top priorities over the next six months.

Organizations that use OKRs see an improvement in employee engagement, a boost in profitability and productivity, and an enhancement in organization alignment. They're also able to gather the data they need to keep a pulse on their organization.

There are four keys to being successful with OKRs as an HR/people leader:

1. **Establish alignment across teams.**

   When employees have a clear line of sight between daily work and bigger-picture goals and objectives, they are more likely to be focused, engaged, and productive. But it's not just individual work that needs to be connected to goals; it's also team and cross-functional work.

   Here are three ways you can establish alignment across teams when establishing OKRs:

   - **Help cross-functional teams work together.** As an HR/people leader, you are already in a position to serve as a strategic advisor and connector of key business units. Use that influence to encourage cross-functional leaders to align on their OKRs from the beginning. That means meeting with each other to discuss priorities before the planning cycle begins.

   - **Hold regular town hall meetings.** These all-hands meetings are an incredible opportunity to ensure that everyone—yes, everyone!—understands the mission, vision, and values of your organization. Keeping these foundational elements of your business top of mind helps ensure that OKRs are aligned with the bigger picture.

   - **Make sure objectives cascade from the top of the organization down to the individual.** If your C-suite leaders are stalling on OKR creation, remind them that the rest of the organization can't be successful until those objectives are set. If leaders always seem to be falling behind, work with your OKR program admin to set automatic calendar reminders in your OKR software solution at key points in the planning cycle.

2. **Ensure transparency across the organization.**

Too many aspects of today's work are being constrained by siloes, from siloed goals to siloed data to siloed knowledge. When these core elements of business are happening in departmental or functional vacuums, it limits an organization's ability to embrace opportunities, address risk, and adapt quickly to change. Transparency is the antidote to siloes. Here's how you can ensure that your OKR program is transparent:

- **Involve all employees.** Even if not all employees are actively creating OKRs, they should all at least be able to see organizational objectives. I've seen retail customers use OKRs for store associates; marketing teams use it for agency partners; web teams use it for external developers; and so much more.

- **Share the "why."** Employees will be more invested in achieving objectives if they understand why they are the priorities for the business or for their team. Openly share the thought process behind these priorities with your own HR team, and encourage other leaders to do the same.

- **Tell people where you're headed.** It's not just transparency around OKRs that's needed, but also about where your OKR program is headed. Change management can be tough, but as an HR/people leader, you have the power to make it easier for your employees. As your OKR program evolves and matures, make sure to send timely and honest communications to your employees so they understand why changes are happening.

3. **Drive individual performance management.**

While it can be tempting to tie OKRs and individual performance together, it's important to remember that OKRs are supposed to be aspirational. That means the progress toward a goal doesn't necessarily correlate to employee performance, and vice versa.

- **Don't tie OKR performance to compensation.** While performance management has its place in connection with objectives and key results, it's important that compensation is not tied to OKR performance. Doing so could hinder employee performance and business growth.

4. **Take point on building a positive employee experience around OKRs.**

It's one thing to get your OKR program up and running, it's another to make sure your entire organization is actively engaged. And yet, it's crucial to the success of your OKR program that every employee is invested and motivated to achieve the objectives that have been set. While front-line managers will absorb much of the day-to-day effort, as chief people officer, you can help drive organization-wide improvements that make the employee experience outstanding.

Here are four tips for how you can help drive the planning process forward as an HR/people leader:

- **Publish an annual calendar.** This way, everyone can see when OKR planning starts, when monthly reviews will happen, and when quarterly scoring and reflection will occur.

- **Hold trainings for managers, team leaders, and individual contributors.** This will ensure that all employees understand how to get the most out of OKRs and OKR software depending on their role.

- **Embrace integrations.** A major benefit of using OKR software for your program is that it allows you to integrate the process into the daily operations of your organization, making updates right in Slack or Teams. This makes checking in on progress a habit and helps drive adoption of OKRs.

Optional Role: Admin/IT

In many ways, admin/IT teams drive the employee experience around an OKR program. 89% of CIOs see themselves as change agents who play a role in improving the culture of their organizations. As an admin/IT employee in a hybrid world, it's essential that you leverage technology to enhance collaboration, productivity, and the employee experience.

And yet, nearly a third of CIOs and CTOs worry about not having the right technology tools to support hybrid work. Successful CIOs understand that their role goes beyond simply choosing and deploying new technology platforms to solve immediate needs. Your guidance and expertise will play a key role in whether the organization meets its objectives as a whole. In other words, your organization will thrive under your leadership when you go beyond tech strategy to encourage alignment of purpose and facilitate execution of overarching organizational goals.

There are four keys to being successful with OKRs as an admin/IT professional:

1. **Establish divisional alignment.**

    Turning strategy into results is not an easy task. Yet, it's easier when your entire organization is aligned around the most important outcomes for the organization in the short and long term. This is what OKRs do; they define where you want to go and how you will get there, and hold everyone accountable for their piece of the puzzle.

    Here are three tips you can use to keep your team focused on outcomes when establishing their OKRs:
    - **Make sure your team agrees on only three to five objectives for each department during any given planning cycle.** Any more than that and you run the

risk of "setting and forgetting" your OKRs. Staying focused will produce the best results.

- **Push back on your managers and leaders if their OKRs don't align with your organization's strategic plan.** You should always be able to clearly map the desired outcome of an objective back to a strategic priority.

- **Make sure there is only one owner for each OKR.** It is common to have multiple teams involved in achieving the same result, but even in those cases, there should only be one clear overall owner in order to enhance accountability.

2. **Guide performance and alignment of technical teams.**

Successful admin/IT professionals prioritize collaboration at the highest levels of the organization. When teams have visibility and understanding of each other's objectives, the organization is better aligned for future growth. Once objectives have been set, it's time to create your key results and key initiatives and projects—how you plan to get to your objectives and key results.

Here are three tips for how you can help to establish and enforce ownership of objectives, key results, key initiatives, and projects:

- Use your OKR software to keep an eye on progress and maintain alignment at the highest levels of your organization. If you notice that an IT objective is falling behind, make time to meet with that OKR owner as soon as possible.

- Hold regular review meetings. Alignment fails when it's not continually reinforced, so make sure your team is meeting at least once a month to check in on OKR progress. You should attend these meetings to help bridge the gap between executive strategy sessions that you are privy to and in-line management.

- When writing key results, use the following formula to ensure that each result can be tracked against a measurement and attached to an action (a key initiative or project). This is how you will assess whether your strategy is working. Key results will most commonly be a measurable metric (a number), although in some cases they are a milestone (a percentage complete). It's preferable to avoid results that can't be measured, like delivery dates or binary (yes/no) metrics.

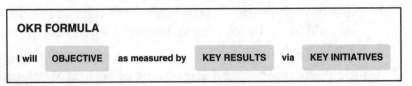

OKR FORMULA

I will   OBJECTIVE   as measured by   KEY RESULTS   via   KEY INITIATIVES

3. **Drive and support global planning cadence for engineers.**
   It's one thing to get your organization's leadership team aligned on key areas of focus for your business, it's another to get them to execute on them. And yet, it's crucial to the success of your OKR program that every team member works toward these goals every day.

   As an admin/IT team, you can influence the culture of your organization and help align organizational strategy to make the connection between strategy and daily work, starting at the highest level. Here are three tips for how you can help create a culture that prioritizes aligned progress:
   - **Be an OKR champion.** Adoption of new methodology requires momentum. An OKR champion provides a consistent push to encourage adoption. Be your organization's OKR champion by continually educating yourself on the ins and outs of OKRs. Share your knowledge at the highest levels and develop plans for successful rollout and maintenance of the OKR program throughout the organization.
   - **Make the OKR planning and tracking easier by automating the process with OKR software.** Consolidating OKR data in one place will help you gain

deep insight into goals across all departments so you can set up objectives for your team that contribute to success across the organization.

- **Prioritize OKR software training.** You are in the unique position to help your organization successfully adopt an OKR software program. You are also the person responsible for making sure they have the right training to make it run smoothly. Make your first OKR objective ensuring that all employees are understanding and using your OKR software.

4. **Take point on agile development execution.**

This year, 43% of CIOs and CTOs are making changes to their strategic plans based on changing business conditions, and that's okay. OKR planning should always be a fluid, agile process. Once OKRs are set, it is your responsibility to ensure that progress is being made in the right direction. Sometimes goals need to change if a more advantageous priority arises, if it becomes clear it isn't feasible, or if you uncover an insight that suggests there should be an adjustment.

The data gathered from these check-ins will provide insight into which goals are cruising along, and which may be at risk of falling behind. With that information in hand, you will know if there's a need to shift directions or whether the strategy is still on course.

Here are three tips for how you can help drive the planning process forward:

- **Take advantage of OKR data to manage resources.** One of the most powerful things about OKRs is that they keep you focused on key priorities. If you see that an OKR is falling off course, you can step in to reallocate resources or to address roadblocks in order to get things back on track.

- **Embrace integrations.** A major benefit of using OKR software for your program is that it allows you to integrate the process into the daily operations of your organization through the communication tools used daily. This makes checking in on progress a habit and helps drive adoption of OKRs.

- **Keep communicating.** Remind your team that they are allowed to change course if needed in order to achieve desired results. OKRs are flexible and should evolve if conditions change. Remembering this can help everyone make progress in the right direction and reduce unproductive work.

23

A Step-by-Step Guide to Getting Started with OKRs

Now that I've broken down the keys to success for OKRs and by each major role in the OKR process, I want to take you through a step-by-step process for getting started with OKRs in your organization.

Step 1: Getting Started with the OKR Maturity Model

Use the OKR maturity model I referenced earlier to determine where your program stands today (or doesn't stand) and the potential for growth that can be yours with the right focus.

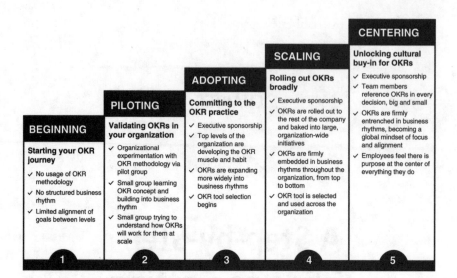

Let me break down the OKR maturity model a bit more granularly for you.

Stage 1 is the **beginning** of your organization's OKR journey. If your organization is in this stage, you're not actively using the OKR methodology today. You may have an existing task management and/or goal-setting system in place at either the organization-wide or team level, but no structured, organization-wide process that's working for everybody.

You may have read a blog post on OKRs and are familiar with the OKR concept, but have little to no experience implementing the framework. You define goals based on a planning cycle of a year or longer. You may struggle with departments sharing goals, progress, and results with one another with a defined cadence. Employees cannot track how their work contributes to specific goals at the department or organization-wide levels.

Stage 2 is the **piloting** stage. In this stage, you are validating OKRs in your organization. You are rolling out a pilot group (more on that in the next step in this section) to iron out the kinks before you roll out to the rest of your organization. This may be at the leadership level, department level, or team level. You are using this time to understand how OKRs will work for you at scale and nail down your rhythms so you can expand to the rest of the organization.

Stage 3 is all about **adopting** OKRs, committing to the OKR practice, and broadening your approach. In this stage, top levels of your organization are developing the OKR muscle and habit, pre-seeding the ideas and philosophies of OKRs with their teams, and beginning to work OKRs into business rhythms like team meetings and collaboratively building company-wide OKRs.

Stage 4 is **scaling**. In this stage, you are rolling out OKRs to your entire organization, embedding in current rituals and creating new ones. You are training up your teams and your OKR tool has been selected.

Stage 5, your ideal state, is OKR **centering**. This is where leadership doesn't have to be in the room for the decisions that reflect your organization's mission, values, strategy, and OKRs to be made. Every employee feels comfortable asking questions like "Which objective does that roll up to?" "Which initiative should I deprioritize to accommodate this new one?" and "What are we hoping our key result will be here?"

In other words, everyone in your organization is so clear on their focus, the specified outcomes of their work and how these align to the teams that surround them, that OKRs have become an organic part of the fabric of the business. Employees feel there is purpose in the work they do and understand the definition of success.

So how should you use the OKR model to get started with OKRs?

- **Using the descriptors above as a guide, identify where your organization sits today.** Before you can get going, you have to be realistic and clear about where you are today.
- **Commit to milestones for getting to each stage in the OKR maturity model.** Use increments of months, quarters, half-years, or even years. Remember that OKR implementation is a long game, taking effort to get it right for your organization and reaping major rewards when you do.
- **Use the maturity model as a framework for initiating and continuing the conversation around OKRs as you roll them out in your organization.** This will help frame up conversations about your organization's current status when it comes to goal-setting, what comes next, and what the ideal state looks like. What does your organization have to do to get from OKR piloting to OKR adopting, for instance?

Now that you know where you are, where you want to go, and your broad timeline, it's time to choose your OKR rollout strategy.

Step 2: Understand the Phases of OKR Rollout

For OKRs to be a successful driving force for your strategy, they need to be baked into your business rhythm. That starts with understanding the necessary phases of a successful rollout.

Give yourself enough time to get it right. Most companies say it takes at least two to three quarters to get their OKR process right, and even then, it's iterative.

When it comes to setting good OKRs, Amanda Nicholson of Formstack says expecting perfection at first is just not realistic. "You have to teach the skill, allow people to set really crappy OKRs, and learn from that experience."

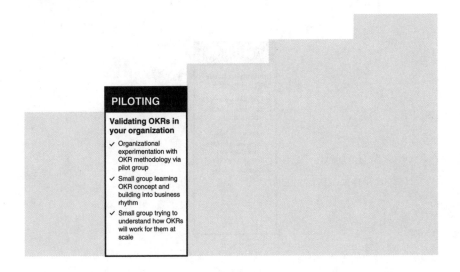

PILOTING

Validating OKRs in your organization

- ✓ Organizational experimentation with OKR methodology via pilot group
- ✓ Small group learning OKR concept and building into business rhythm
- ✓ Small group trying to understand how OKRs will work for them at scale

Phase 2: Leadership-Only Pilot

I recommend rolling out your OKR program systematically from the top down, starting with a pilot program. The benefit of this method is that employees see that senior leadership is fully behind the program, serving as a model example for the program's importance, and any issues can be worked out before expanding the program to the entire company.

In the first quarter of launch, OKRs are set by the executive team and the entire organization has access to view long-term, strategic goals even without team and department OKRs. Throughout the quarter, a weekly cadence for check-ins is set as an example, and meeting agendas are structured around measurement against these goals.

Last, after another one or two quarters, team managers expand their key results another level down to individual team members.

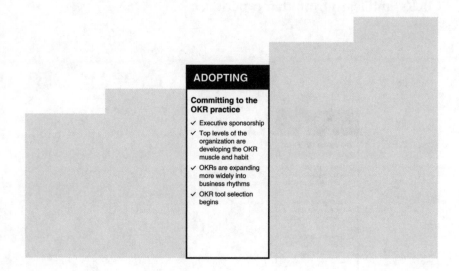

Phase 3: Leadership and Departments

After a successful first quarter (or two), goals are cascaded one level down to departments. Those OKRs should be aligned with the senior leadership team. This is your adopting stage in the OKR maturity model.

This department adopts a weekly cadence for check-ins for one to two quarters, experimenting with what works and making changes as necessary. Along the way, department-level leaders report back to the executive sponsor and OKR champion regarding successes, challenges, and recommendations.

Once the executive team and department-level leaders are comfortable with how the program is working, a training plan is formulated to roll out OKRs at the team level.

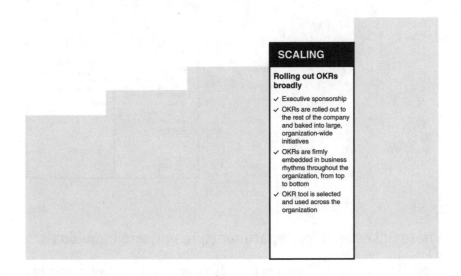

SCALING

Rolling out OKRs broadly

✓ Executive sponsorship
✓ OKRs are rolled out to the rest of the company and baked into large, organization-wide initiatives
✓ OKRs are firmly embedded in business rhythms throughout the organization, from top to bottom
✓ OKR tool is selected and used across the organization

Phase 4: Leadership, Departments, and Teams

Now that you have implemented OKRs at the leadership level and department level, it's time to roll out OKRs to individual teams. You are in the scaling stage of the OKR maturity model.

It is vital that you equip team managers and teams at this point with the OKR training they need to understand how to write, track, and measure OKRs.

Remember that the first step within this phase is to have team managers build team-level OKRs collaboratively with their team members. Once this process is going smoothly and widely understood by team members, it's time to move on to the next and final phase of OKR rollout: bringing in individual OKRs.

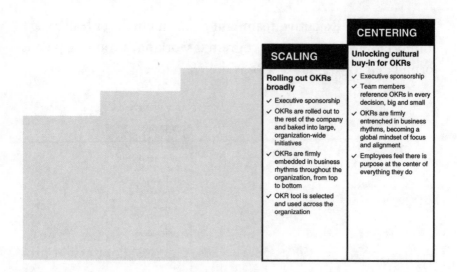

Phase 5: Leadership, Departments, Teams, and Individuals

This final phase sits somewhere between scaling and centering on the OKR maturity model, with centering being the ideal end state of this phase.

In this phase, you roll out OKRs to individuals on the level of the key initiatives and projects they are working on, so that they have a full understanding of how their daily work is contributing to their team-wide OKRs, department-level OKRs, and company-level OKRs.

Because individual team members should already be familiar with the OKR process from collaborating on writing their team-level OKRs and the previous OKR evangelization from executive leadership and department-level leaders, this final phase should feel natural.

To support individual team members in this phase, do the following:

- Widely communicate what company-level, department-level, and team-level OKRs are so that individual team members understand how to connect their OKRs to the big picture.

- Schedule specific trainings/coaching sessions for coming up with individual OKRs.
- As a team manager, check in regularly with team members in 1:1s to find out how the OKR writing process is going.
- Use your OKR software tool to keep tabs on OKR progress and roadblocks throughout the quarter.

One final note here: if your organization does not want to roll out OKRs from leadership down, you can adopt a pilot program model instead for initial rollout.

In this model, individual departments (for example, the marketing or IT department, or a product engineering team) do a top-to-bottom rollout involving team managers and individual employees. Here's how it goes:

1. With support of upper management, the group adopts a weekly cadence for check-ins for one to two quarters, experimenting with what works and making agile changes. Along the way, team managers report back to management regarding successes, challenges, and recommendations.
2. Once the individual department and management are comfortably in a rhythm, a training plan is formulated to roll out OKRs to the rest of the organization.

No matter which type of pilot program you choose, it's important to find out what works best for your organization. Be patient, as it usually takes a few quarters to get comfortable with change. Soon, though, you will get into a solid rhythm and your OKR program will grow and mature naturally alongside your organization.

Now let's move on to step 3, the bread and butter of getting started with OKRs: putting together your project plan and communication plan.

Step 3: Put Together Your Project Plan and Communication Plan

While it's common for OKR programs to vary from company to company, once your phased rollout of OKRs is complete, a typical OKR cycle looks like this:

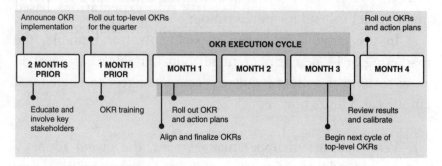

The Typical OKR Cycle

Here are the project milestones you should hit to ensure that everyone in your organization is aware of what's happening and what is expected of them.

Milestone 1: Kickoff Meeting to Announce OKR Implementation

The first milestone of implementation is the same as it would be for any major initiative: you host a kickoff meeting. This meeting is generally set at the leadership level but includes your OKR champion and department-level heads as well.

The goal of this meeting is to define the parameters of the initial launch and create an action plan among the key stakeholders involved.

I generally recommend people use a responsibility matrix like RACI (responsible, accountable, consulted, informed) or RAPID (recommend, agree, perform, input, decide) when building this plan. Your OKR program is about establishing accountability, and that is hard to do without creating accountability from the start.

There will be three items to focus on in this meeting:

1. **Assemble the team and clarify role expectations** based on the key roles we outlined earlier in this chapter.

2. **Define OKR rollout milestones and next steps.** Here is a sample of what a milestone timeline might look like for the leadership team phase.

3. **Set expectations.** No matter which phase you're in—leadership team rollout, department rollout, team rollout, or individual rollout—make sure the following is clear:
   - What is expected of each role
   - Due dates for all members of the participating team
   - When and how feedback will be requested and incorporated

Milestone 2: Define Your Company-Level OKR Strategy and Communications Plan

Your company-level OKRs are developed top-down, defined at the executive level, and must be an integral part of the company culture, championed throughout the year.

PHASE 1: LEADERSHIP TEAM 30-60-90 OKR ROLLOUT
End-to-end view of the leadership team OKR rollout

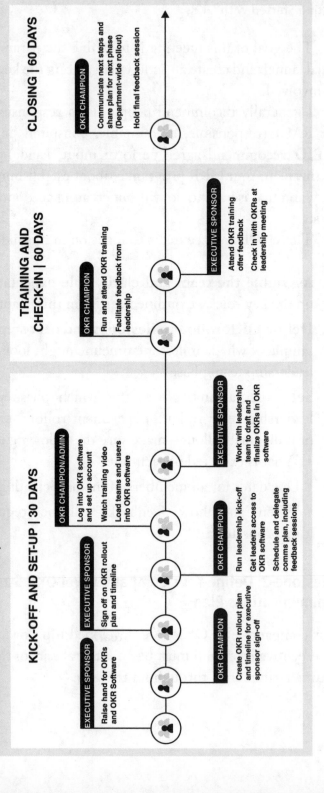

KICK-OFF AND SET-UP | 30 DAYS

EXECUTIVE SPONSOR
Raise hand for OKRs and OKR Software

EXECUTIVE SPONSOR
Sign off on OKR rollout plan and timeline

OKR CHAMPION
Create OKR rollout plan and timeline for executive sponsor sign-off

OKR CHAMPION
Run leadership kick-off
Get leaders access to OKR software
Schedule and delegate comms plan, including feedback sessions

OKR CHAMPION/ADMIN
Log into OKR software and set up account
Watch training video
Load teams and users into OKR software

EXECUTIVE SPONSOR
Work with leadership team to draft and finalize OKRs in OKR software

TRAINING AND CHECK-IN | 60 DAYS

OKR CHAMPION
Run and attend OKR training
Facilitate feedback from leadership

EXECUTIVE SPONSOR
Attend OKR training offer feedback
Check in with OKRs at leadership meeting

CLOSING | 60 DAYS

OKR CHAMPION
Communicate next steps and share plan for next phase (Department-wide rollout)
Hold final feedback session

Once you have completed your leadership team rollout, it is time to take the lessons you have learned and define your communications plan for department-wide and team-wide rollout.

Even if you don't have the goals set down to the specific metrics, at least being very transparent and clear about the direction the organization is taking is very important and that is a tremendous value OKRs bring. These company objectives will set the tone for the OKRs created and work done throughout the company.

Sample Communications Plan

The emails you send to your company or department (depending on how widely you are rolling out OKRs) should address the following questions to ensure that your vision is communicated, expectations are set, and questions are answered preemptively.

Company-Level or Department-Level Communications
Email #1: OKRs + Vision

Audience: Entire company or department

Voice: Executive sponsor

- What are OKRs?
- Why are we transitioning to OKRs?
- Where are OKRs going to take our company?
- What does that mean for you?

(continued)

Email #2: Vision + Expectations

Audience: Entire company or department

Voice: OKR champion

- Who will be involved in the OKR process?
- What are OKR champions?
- Why are we investing in OKR champions?
- When do we use OKRs?
- How does this change our current planning process?
- Why are we moving to an OKR platform?
- What are the expectations for using the platform?

Email #3: Rollout Plan

Audience: Entire company or department

Voice: OKR champion

- How are we planning to roll out OKRs?
- What are the key deadlines?

Email #4: Company OKRs + OKR Resources

Audience: Entire company or department

Voice: OKR champion

- What are our company OKRs?
- What are the expectations for what we now do with the company OKRs?
- How should we align our OKRs?
- Where can we go to learn more about OKRs?
- How can I get help on my OKRs?

Email #5: OKR Finalization

Audience: Entire company or department

Voice: OKR champion

- Are all of our OKRs finalized?
- Where can we find our OKRs?

Email #6: Checking in on OKRs

Audience: Entire company or department

Voice: OKR champion

- How often should we be checking in on OKRs?
- What does a good check-in look like?
- When should we be talking about our OKRs?

Email #7: Reflection, Scoring, and Planning

Audience: Entire company or department

Voice: OKR champion

- When do we score and reflect on our OKRs?
- How are we expected to reflect on our OKRs?
- What are the deadlines for scoring and next quarter's planning?

Email #8: OKR Results + Learnings

Audience: Entire company or department

Voice: OKR champion

- What were the main results of our OKRs?
- What are we celebrating?
- What did we learn from this first OKR cycle?

Milestone 3: Roll Out Top-Level OKRs for the Quarter

Once the high-level strategy is set, it's time to bring the rest of the organization into the conversation for feedback, and to begin the next level of planning.

Don't be surprised if this is iterative. You'll learn about dependencies, risks, and opportunities that the original planning sessions may not have surfaced.

"For the overall company or organization, start with the annual and then develop the quarterly OKRs," says Intel Alumni Association president Howard Jacob. "Group and team OKRs derive from these quarterly OKRs, and most of the individual OKRs derive from the group/team OKRs. Individuals may also create career/personal development OKRs for the year, which then get implemented quarterly.

"For example, completing external training or education goals to prepare them for their next promotion or project, or becoming an internal trainer/mentor/coach to help develop both their skills and those of their peers, could be appropriate individual OKRs."

There are three activities that happen within the context of this milestone:

1. Assign key results for corporate objectives to the appropriate teams.
2. Teams respond to assigned corporate key results by drafting their OKRs with senior leadership support.
3. Collaborate with team leaders and stakeholders for feedback.

Milestone 4: OKR Training and Enablement (Champion Team OKR Launch)

As you get closer to organization-wide implementation, training and enablement are critical.

This is where the OKR champion takes the reins and makes sure everyone knows their role and is armed with the proper context, framework, and even excitement about what's to come. The champion will facilitate OKR training for all levels of employees, identifying stakeholders and specific needs.

It's helpful to break training sessions into groups, as the information needed and level of involvement will differ:

- Company leadership and OKR champions
- Managers and department leads
- All employees/individuals
- Geographical and logistical grouping (if applicable)

With these groups, you'll need to address three things:

1. Discuss existing goal-setting methods and how the OKR framework differs.
2. Develop coaching and training plan for those involved.
3. Set coaching and training schedule.

Milestone 5: Align and Finalize OKRs (All-Employee OKR Launch)

The fifth milestone is to have the entire company align and finalize their OKRs. This is a critical step because if it's approached with half-measures, OKRs will be seen as "another thing we have to do" by the broader team. There will always be a contingent of detractors who just don't "get it" so be prepared for that, and be brutally honest with yourself about how people will respond, but also set yourself up for success by creating the right structure to add value to every employee.

This milestone is marked by cascading objectives to individuals in a process that loosely goes like this (add deadlines, meetings, and process as you see fit).

- High-level OKRs flow downward to business units, team leads, managers, and eventually individuals.
- Team members digest and respond with individual OKRs.
- Managers review and iterate OKRs with team members.
- OKRs are reviewed and finalized to ensure organizational alignment.

From here, cross-company collaboration between team leaders and stakeholders for feedback will be necessary in order to iterate, refine, and finalize company-level OKRs.

Milestone 6: Roll Out OKRs and Action Plan

Milestone 6 marks the operationalization of an OKR program, including a definition of the ongoing rhythm.

- Define and schedule company-wide review cadence.
- Clearly communicate cadence and set expectations.
- OKR execution begins.

As you move through your OKR rollout, be sure to build in plenty of touchpoints, including meetings and anonymous forms, to get feedback from everyone involved in the process. Reflect regularly on what you're learning and how you are going to incorporate the feedback so that participants understand that this is an iterative process and they are key contributors, whether they are members of leadership, team managers, or individual contributors.

Step 4: Coach Your Group on Developing Great OKRs

In Chapter 9, I shared an interactive workshop to developing great OKRs. During Step 4, you'll put that workshop into action.

Step 5: Integrate OKRs into Your Business Rhythms

One of the most common pitfalls that companies face when adopting an OKR program is setting OKRs but failing to establish a rhythm for checking in with them and embedding them into the DNA of the organization. Just as an orchestra needs a conductor to guide them through their performance, so too does a business need a rhythm to guide them through their goal setting.

Without this rhythm in place, it can be difficult to make OKRs stick. And if OKRs don't stick, then you won't reap the rewards of the OKR methodology, and you'll be less likely to achieve your goals.

If you want your OKR program to be successful, then it's time to start thinking about how you will keep your organization on track throughout the planning cycle. From daily check-ins to quarterly reviews to end-of-cycle reflection and scoring, these milestones will become your OKR rhythm. When fully incorporated into your OKR program, these elements are what will inform and drive the execution and adoption of this methodology.

Brainstorming Exercise: Assess Your Current Rhythm

Before you begin building your new OKR rhythm, consider your existing one. You may already have a system in place to check in on progress toward goals.

- What milestone activities do you think are important for your organization to stay aligned and empowered?
- Are they working?
- Can they be improved?
- Are there others that could be added into the 3C (create, check-in, close) framework?

With an OKR program, you'll likely need to implement a more consistent and frequent cadence of check-ins and reviews than what you're currently doing. However, there may still be elements of your existing processes that you can draw on. Take some time to assess what works well in your current state, and how you can carry that forward to your OKR program.

> **TIP:** Most organizations choose to establish a quarterly cadence for their OKRs, but it is possible to shorten or extend this timeline as needed to suit the needs of your company.

Building Out Your OKR Rhythm

Let's now start to outline the rhythm for your OKR program.

For those on a quarterly cadence (again, that's the case for most organizations), your timeline will look like this:

MONTH ONE				MONTH TWO				MONTH THREE				M 4
W 1	W 2	W 3	W 4	W 5	W 6	W 7	W 8	W 9	W 10	W 11	W 12	W 1

CREATE

CHECK-IN

CLOSE

Notice that the 3 Cs are clearly present in this rhythm. Next, I break them down one by one so you can execute this rhythm at your organization.

Phase 1: Create

Before and during Week 1 of the quarter, you'll be creating your OKRs.

Here are your key milestones during this phase.

Milestone 1 (Seven Days before Week 1): Draft and Share Company OKRs Seven days before a new quarter begins, you and your leadership team will meet to draft OKRs, reflect, and prioritize. Ask these questions to help narrow your list of potential objectives down to just three to five:

- **What went well last quarter?** Why?
- **Where do we have room for improvement?** How?

- **What should be our focus going forward?** Why?
- **Will focusing here get us closer to our vision?** Is it in line with our mission and values?

Milestone 2 (Five Days before Week 1): OKR Drafting and Editing Sessions for Teams and Departments Once company-wide OKRs are set, share them with department heads and team leaders. Remember, OKRs are meant to cascade down from the highest level of your organization in order to build alignment. Thus, it is critical to share company-wide OKRs transparently to everyone within your organization.

Milestone 3 (Week 1): Finalize and Load OKRs into Your OKR Tool By the end of week 1, your leaders and teams should all have finalized and loaded their OKRs into your OKR tool.

Now let's move to the check-in phase.

Phase 2: Check In

Milestone 1: Weave Frequent Check-Ins into Existing Rhythms
Frequent check-ins help leaders keep a pulse on the health of their goals. Are they still tracking to reach them on time? Is there a roadblock or an unanticipated factor that will require the plan to change? Consider providing some of these discussion questions to leaders to guide their thinking for their first meeting and encourage them to use their dashboards to conduct meetings.

Review sessions increase focus, accountability, autonomy, and transparency throughout the organization. Without these sessions, you risk losing sight of your goals and working in silos, disconnected from the big picture.

But with a close eye on progress and a dedicated process for learning and improvement, review sessions will result in increased alignment, a stronger organizational culture, and greater performance in the future.

OKR reviews come in all shapes and sizes—from morning check-ins to weekly team meetings to quarterly business reviews.

I recommend weaving OKR reviews and check-ins into the meetings you already have on the books to avoid increased meeting load but maintain a close eye on how you are tracking with OKRs.

Here are four specific meetings you can incorporate OKRs into, and one new meeting I recommend:

1. **Weekly internal leadership meetings** (executive, department, and team manager levels)

     Weave OKR check-ins and reminders into weekly leadership meetings for executives, department heads, and team managers, respectively.

     Connecting every department with OKRs reinforces that OKRs should be top of mind and drive the work being done to help your organization reach its goals.

     Including OKRs in meetings for team managers helps eliminate silos; if there are issues, they can be addressed more efficiently.

     At the end of the quarter, use this meeting as an opportunity to go over what went wrong, what went right, and what the plan is for the future quarter.

2. **Company-wide meetings**

     Company leaders should incorporate OKRs into their regular company-wide meetings and town halls as a part of the discussion around important updates or issues the company is having. The state of the company should be driven by where OKR progress stands. This is also a great opportunity for employees to participate by asking questions and making suggestions.

3. Team-level meetings

OKRs should be a part of every team-level meeting that a team manager holds. They should be baked into the structure of team meetings in the following ways:
- As a collaborative ideation session prior to the new quarter to ensure team engagement and buy-in.
- As part of the regular structure of round robin updates.
- As a formalized check-in at the beginning, midway, and end of a quarter.

4. 1:1s

OKRs should make a regular appearance at 1:1s between team managers and team members, using your OKR software as a facilitating mechanism. OKRs should be baked into these 1:1s in the following ways:
- Checking in on individual progress.
- Identifying roadblocks and gaps, and helping to clear them as a manager.
- Sharing context about how company-wide OKRs are influencing team priorities and individual priorities.

5. Quarterly cross-functional OKR meetings (New)

There is one new meeting that I recommend, and it's a cross-functional one. This meeting is necessary because it is directly related to the core value of OKRs: ensuring cross-functional visibility and alignment.

Once a quarter, plan a cross-functional meeting with stakeholders who own a piece of each OKR. For example, if you have an objective around 10x revenue growth, you could hold a quarterly meeting with sales, customer service, marketing, and product stakeholders who have cascaded OKRs supporting that topic.

This meeting will help you identify wins, flaws, and lessons for the future in both the OKRs you come up with and the OKR process itself.

Phase 3: Close and Score

Now it's time to see how you performed!

Milestone 1: Score and Close   Before the quarter ends, ask your OKR solution to send out automatic reminders to ensure that all participating departments and teams complete final check-ins, then close and score their OKRs.

Remind **EXECUTIVES** begin closing out OKRs **2 WEEKS** before quarter-end

Remind **DEPARTMENT HEADS** begin closing out OKRs **1 WEEK** before quarter-end

Remind **TEAM MANAGERS** begin closing out OKRs **2 DAYS** before quarter-end

Milestone 2: Review and Move Forward

During the last week of the quarter, you'll be doing two things simultaneously: closing out the current quarter's OKRs and finalizing the OKRs for the upcoming quarter.

The good news is, one thing informs the other. Spend the first half of your OKR meeting in the last week reflecting on what went well and what didn't go well.

Take time to consider whether or not you are going to carry forward any unfinished OKRs into the next quarter. Next, spend the second half of the meeting using the lessons learned to inform your priorities for the upcoming quarter. Update any carry-forward OKRs to reflect these learnings so you can learn, iterate, and achieve your goal next time around.

Conclusion

Let's say you're trying to build the perfect OKR. Your objective is aspirational and lofty: Build the tallest building in the world.

This is the goal they set for the Empire State Building. The Empire State Building, impressively, was finished 12 days early and came in at $20 million under budget.

Another example of a perfect OKR is the one for the Golden Gate Bridge. The objective: Build the longest suspension bridge in the world. And, like the Empire State Building, the Golden Gate Bridge came in ahead of schedule and $1.3 million under budget.

Unfortunately, those are the exceptions. There's a long history of poor planning that spans major projects like this across the globe. Let's look at a couple of examples, like the Quebec Bridge.

The Quebec Bridge was budgeted for $6 million and ended up costing $23 million. It took 30 years to build and collapsed twice during the process.

The Sydney Opera House was budgeted for $7 million and came in at over $100 million. It was also 10 years late.

The James Webb telescope saw a similar fate, racking up a 1900% cost overrun. The telescope finished well behind schedule when it launched at the end of 2021.

My favorite example is the Second Avenue subway system in New York City. Originally, the system was budgeted at $99 million. It's now at $17 billion! Just a slight difference. It was proposed in 1929 and set to finish in 2029—100 years late.

In *The Oxford Handbook of Megaproject Management* by Bent Flyvbjerg, "the iron law of mega projects" is: they will come in over budget, over time, and under benefits, over and over again.

Flyvbjerg and his team studied 100 years of data on the subject, and found that 90% of projects came in over budget, over time, and under benefits again and again and again.

This phenomenon isn't exclusive to government projects, either. The researchers talked to students and asked them, "How long do you think it will take to finish your thesis?" They guessed 34 days, with the true outcome of 56 days.

If I'm being honest, I expected to finish this book much quicker than I did, as well.

$55 billion a year is lost to project delays, and there's a one-in-six chance that the project will be 200% over budget.

Take Justin Rosenstein, for example. Justin worked for Google. He has a brilliant mind for products. He co-invented Google Chat. While he was at Google, he realized the extent of these planning problems and he built out some planning software. It didn't take off.

Later on, he went over to Facebook and he couldn't bring that software with him. He invented the Like button and built *new* planning software to make things more efficient.

Finally, he left Facebook to start his own company, called Asana, and he built the project planning software again. By his third time building planning software, you'd think he'd be a pro.

He did, too, so he predicted that the product would be launched within a year. And even the founder of a project planning company took three years to launch the company.

What is this phenomenon? And why does it happen? It's the planning fallacy, which is a tendency to underestimate the time, costs, and risk of future actions, and there are three reasons for it.

Optimism

The first reason is optimism. It's wishful thinking to focus on the best possible scenario and what you want to happen as opposed to past experience. This optimism is a double-edged sword, because it can motivate you and inspire you to take on bigger and more ambitious challenges, but it can also lead to poor planning and missed objectives.

Bias

The second reason is a self-serving bias. When something in the past has been successful, you tend to take the credit for yourself, but if it's a failure, you try to blame it on other things. You remember your wins in a more positive light than your losses. "It would have worked if it weren't for . . ."

Coordination Neglect

The third reason for the planning fallacy is coordination neglect. You would think that as a project starts to get late, your instinct would tell you to bring more resources into the fold to get it done and make it go faster. What researchers have actually found is that bringing more parties into a project late in the game can hurt the deadline more than it helps, because it takes time and bandwidth away from the current team to spin up the new members.

How Can You Get Around the Planning Fallacy?

Things are almost always going to take longer than you think, but you can use OKRs to help alleviate that aspect of the planning fallacy.

OKRs help you and your team focus. Instead of the five or 10 things you *think* you can do, you reduce that down to three to five that you can really get right. This focus enables a strong planning process and the permission to say no to distractions.

OKRs also bring transparency and provide accountability and collaboration, where everyone across the company (or a specific project) can see what's going on. What Flyvbjerg found is that you're more likely to incorrectly predict your own tasks. By leveraging OKRs' inherent transparency, you're able to involve stakeholders as checks and balances from the first step. When you look at other people's projects, you're more skeptical. You can say, "Hmm, that looks like it might take a little longer than you're planning."

Finally, OKRs help you make data-driven decisions. You're going to use these OKRs to track progress toward key milestones, and over time, you'll build up a data set of past projects that can inform future ones. This practice keeps you from blindly making timeline predictions, looking forward. Instead, you review past data to set realistic planning goals, based on projects that were similar.

Projects are almost always going to take longer than you think. So whether you have a really ambitious objective, like building the world's largest suspension bridge, or the next software release that you're trying to get out the door, lean on OKRs to bring focus, transparency, and data to your project.

As you continue building your OKR program, you produce a workforce that asks questions like "Does this align to our objective?" and "How is the work I'm doing impacting our organization's outcomes?" You are able to stretch toward ambitious objectives that align to your mission and values, and get crisp about both defining success and connecting output to outcomes.

As OKRs become more entrenched in your organizational culture, you move up the OKR maturity curve.

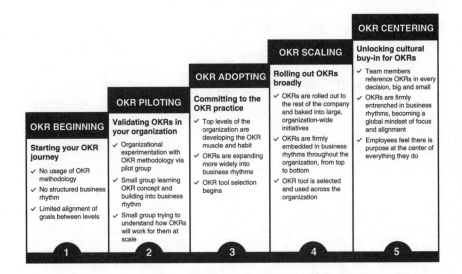

My hope is that this book has answered the questions I set out to answer about OKRs as a goal-setting framework and tool: what OKRs are, why you should implement them in your own organization, how you should roll them out, and when and where to begin.

But my true objective is that you will use the OKR knowledge in this book to turn your most ambitious visions and strategies into reality—on time, within scope, and as a team with a shared purpose.

Acknowledgments

I want to thank, first and foremost, my team, who is constantly striving to learn more about how OKRs help our customers.

Thank you, as well, to our partners, who provided guidance and contributed expertise to this book, and our industry as a whole.

Thank you to my family, for supporting the chaotic life of a startup founder.

Thank you to the investors and supporters who have become a support system stronger than I could ask for.

About the Author

Vetri Vellore is a serial entrepreneur with a proven track record and more than 25 years of experience in building successful products and businesses and has helped thousands of leaders and teams leverage the OKR framework. He is the corporate vice president of Microsoft Viva Goals, after an acquisition of the monumentally successful OKR software company, Ally.io. At Ally, Vetri was CEO and founder, helping thousands of businesses successfully adopt the OKR methodology.

Organizations today operate in a new world in which agility, alignment, and transparency are critical to business success. This realization hit hard when Vetri began scaling his previous startup and discovered the OKR framework, a simple yet powerful model for improving organizational agility, alignment, focus, and transparency. He says:

Being a business leader working to improve team alignment, focus, and engagement towards the strategic priorities of the business, I quickly realized the simple and effective OKR methodology had an amazing ability to accelerate business when implemented well, but I also found that implementing OKRs takes focus and dedication. This prompted me to learn as much as I could about where businesses struggle, and I ultimately founded Ally.io, where we helped solve those problems for leaders across every industry.

The acquisition by Microsoft was a homecoming for Vetri. Prior to founding two SaaS businesses, he led product and engineering teams at Microsoft. He turned around the $200-million-plus systems management enterprise software business, and he led the Visual Studio platform team, managed the partner ecosystem, and shipped several award-winning products over his 14-year tenure at Microsoft.

Vetri is a father of two, and lives with his family in Sammamish, Washington.

Index